TRENCH 31

Clive Ward

DEDICATION

For my Great Uncle, Private Bertram Allen Ward of the 10th Battalion Sherwood Foresters.

Lest we forget.

By Clive Ward

The Unnamed Soldiers
Army Barmy
Bumpers & Bed Blocks
EndEx
EndEx 2 Uncut
You Wouldn't Belize It
The Goat Killer
Homeless Free as a Bird

Writing with Elaine Ward

Half Day Closing
In Sympathy

ACKNOWLEDGMENTS

I'd like to thank my wife and family for their constant support. Big thanks go out to Lynn Lawson for her patience and understanding whilst editing the manuscript.

Chapter 1

Ypres Cemetery, Belgium, 14th February 1966

We arrived at the cemetery near Ypres and we couldn't have picked a better day for our visit. The sky was blue, the surrounding countryside was a sea of green and the birds were in full voice. However, fifty years ago, on this same date, the day had been very different. It had taken my mother, Charlotte Anne Butler, half a century to come to terms with her loss and now she was about to attend the grave for the first time.

We pulled into the car park and sat in silence, gazing out through the window at the expanse of graves. After a while, my mother spoke.

'I'm ready now, might as well get it over and done with eh ducky.'

She always called me ducky. Being Derbyshire born and bred, my mother called everyone ducky.

The grave was a short distance away. Its gravestone stood alongside those of many hundreds of others that signified soldiers and airmen who had given their lives. This is where he was buried. A place of peace, where just a mere fraction of Britain's honoured dead lay resting forever.

I knew where the grave was. I'd been here before, a few years ago on my own. I turned my mother's wheelchair around so that she faced the grave stone, one amongst so many. My mother didn't say a word, she just sat in her wheelchair in silence with tears running slowly down her face. I took a few steps back and lit a cigarette, leaving her alone with her thoughts. I felt sad, but I also felt very proud of the sacrifice that this man and his comrades had made for our country. My mother held a silver locket in her hand, she clasped it tightly and began to weep openly. This was the silver locket that she had worn around her neck since that day in 1916 when it was returned to her. My mother always said that the day they came and told her he'd been killed in action had been bad enough but receiving the locket had been even worse.

Mother wasn't on her own, thousands of families had received the same sad news. The awful notification that their loved ones had been cut down in their prime before they'd had a chance to live their lives, and for what? So many bodies were never found. The Sherwood Foresters alone, lost eleven thousand four hundred and nine men during active service, the vast majority of them on the Western Front.

15[th]of February 1916

Immediately north of Ypres, near the Comines Canal at a stretch of ground known as the Bluff. The poor bastards never stood a chance.

There were so many hazards, exploding artillery shells, snipers and grenades. If they thought the craters were a safe place to take cover from the mayhem, they would have to think again. Those craters became so waterlogged that men could easily sink and drown in the swamp, never to be seen again. Heavy and prolonged rain had turned the landscape into a sea of lethal mud. Now only the dead and the dying littered No Man's Land.

During a lull in the constant bombardment that had started a few days earlier and whilst a dense fog covered No Man's Land, both sides sent out stretcher bearers to retrieve what was left of the dead and wounded. The stench from the bodies strewn across the divide rose up from the ground to assault the senses of the living.

Two British stretcher bearers scrambled from place to place, availing themselves of every shell hole, clinging to whatever cover they could find, calling out to the wounded. The work of the stretcher bearers went on day and night and even under fire these brave men went out to rescue their wounded comrades.

The two stretcher bearers came across yet another body, a member of the 10th Battalion, Sherwood Foresters, lying alongside the bodies of his dead opponents.

'Oh, bloody hell look at this poor bugger, is that who I think it is? I was wondering what had happened to him, at least his body is complete, not like the rest of them.'

A second soldier, a Corporal, knelt down to see if there was any sign of life.

'It looks like he died quickly, a shot to the head, unlike the rest of them.'

Most soldiers died from such dreadful injuries that it was more or less impossible to identify them or find complete bodies to provide a proper burial. Some died slowly, alone and helpless in No Man's Land. Their cries for help would go on for hours, gradually weakening until they were no more.

'What's that he's holding in his hand Corporal?'

The Corporal prised open the hand of the dead soldier.

'It's some sort of locket I think.'

The corporal opened the locket to reveal a photograph of a beautiful smiling young girl.

'Look at that Fred, such a bloody shame, look at her. She's got some bad news coming her way.'

'Come on, let's head back, this is the last one for today, the rest will have to wait. The fog is starting to lift, we don't want to join them do we.'

The two soldiers lifted the body onto the stretcher and headed for the safety of their own lines.

Chapter 2

Eighteen months earlier

On a hot summer evening, in a lush green field, at a place called Parker's Piece in Derby, a young courting couple lay in each other's arms, making the most of their time alone together.

It was August 1914 and Archibald Butler had just turned nineteen years old. War had not long broken out and Archie, along with most of his childhood friends had answered Kitchener's call after seeing the famous posters that encouraged them to join up. In just eight weeks, over three-quarters of a million men in Britain had been recruited for the army. In one month's time, Archie would be joining the newly formed 10th Battalion of the Sherwood Foresters Regiment as an Infantry soldier. Archie was the youngest son of Jack Butler, a hospital porter, and his wife, Bridget Butler, a nurse.

'Aren't you scared Archie?' Charlotte asked.

'Scared of what?' Archie replied frowning.

'You know, the war and what you might have to face out there.'

'Nah, me, never. I'll wager you we don't even see any action, it'll be over by Christmas, that's what they're all saying, you'll see Charlotte.'

'I hope so. You're so brave Archie, my Archie,' said Charlotte. 'And if you do have to fight you'd better look after yourself, don't you go getting too brave!' Charlotte warned him sternly.

'Bloody hell Charlotte! I swear I don't know what'll be worse, facing the Hun or facing you if I don't look after myself!'

Charlotte gave him a playful slap as they embraced once again. They lay on their backs, staring up at the cloudless blue sky.

'I want to give you something Archie, I've been saving up for it. As soon as I saw it, I had to have it. I bought it from a stall in the Market Hall at the weekend.'

Charlotte sat up, leaned over and swung a locket and chain above Archie's head. With the sun in his eyes, he couldn't make out what it was at first. Archie sat up and took the locket in his hands.

'Open it then,' Charlotte urged him.

Archie opened the locket and smiled.

'Do you like it Archie? Do tell me you like it, it's a picture of me.'

'I know it's a picture of you, silly. There isn't anyone as beautiful as you Charlotte. It must have cost you a fair few shillings. How much did you pay for it?'

'Archie, you don't ask questions like that, it's rude. It doesn't matter how much it cost. I want you to wear it always and never take it off, promise me, it'll keep you safe.'

'Thank you, it's lovely, I will Charlotte. I promise.'

Archie smiled, leant towards her and kissed her on the lips, then held her close.

'Thank you, I'll wear it forever.'

Archie then looked at his watch. 'It's getting late Charlotte, it's time for you to head home, or your brother and father will be on the war path.'

'You're right, I'm sorry that my brother is a little over protective Archie, he's a really good person when you get to know him you know.'

'I'm sure he is, after all he's only doing what I'd do, looking out for his little sister.'

Archie was from a large family and was the youngest of the seven offspring. He had two sisters and four brothers and all four of his older brothers worked at the local foundry. Archie had also been working at the foundry since he was fifteen but he wanted more than that. Archie wanted to see the world, so he volunteered to join up, thinking it could be his only chance to get out of his home town of Derby and go places.

Glancing over his shoulder Archie caught sight of two figures in the distance. Charlotte's older brother

David and David's best mate, Bertie, were walking up the embankment towards them.

At twenty-two, David was the oldest child of the Manning family. At six feet three and powerfully built, David Manning was someone you definitely didn't want to get on the wrong side of. His sister, Charlotte, was eighteen, and his brother, Michael, was fifteen and still at school. David had just finished his apprenticeship as a butcher when the call came.

'Maybe it's time that we left, Charlotte,' suggested Archie, nodding his head in the direction of the approaching two men. 'Your brother doesn't look best pleased.'

Charlotte and Archie stood up and brushed themselves down. It wasn't long before David reached them and had Archie in a firm grip.

'Let go of my shirt David Manning, right now!'

David began to push Archie around like a school ground bully.

'Let go - or what? Tell me, what are you going to do little boy?'

'You think I'm scared of you, well I'm not,' stated Archie, sounding more confident that he felt.

Charlotte pushed her way between them.

'Stop it David, leave him alone, he hasn't done anything to you and he's not a little boy, you're the one who's behaving like a little boy, so grow up. Tell him to stop please Bertie,' Charlotte pleaded with her brother's friend.

'Yes, let go of him old man,' Bertie said.

Bertram Ward (Bertie) detested violence of any kind. At school, he always stood up to the bullies, but having his best friend David around to watch his back helped.

At the age of just twelve, Bertram often gave sermons at the local Church. He could speak Latin and left school the top of his class. Bertram was destined for the top, until the war interrupted his progress. Bertram also had a habit of questioning authority, which often got him into trouble.

'What have I told you about seeing my sister? I have a good mind to give you a bloody good hiding,' threatened David.

'Take your hands off me, I can do what I want, and anyway you're not her father.'

Just as a fight looked certain to break out between them, they were all stopped short by the sound of a passing train.

'That'll be the sixteen-forty-five from Crewe, if I'm not mistaken,' said Bertram looking at his pocket watch.

The train was packed with troops and some of the men waved from the windows of the carriages as it trundled slowly towards Derby Station.

'I wonder where they are going?' said Charlotte.

'They're off to the front most probably, just like me and you will be, eh Bertie,' said David proudly.

The long line of train carriages chugged away into the distance and out of sight.

'So, you've both joined up then?' Archie asked.

'We report to Normanton Barracks next month, it's probably the worst decision I've ever made in my short life because God knows what I've let myself in for,' Bertram replied.

'Will you stop worrying Bertie, nothing will happen to you, you're with me remember, so you'll be alright,' assured David.

When the First World War broke out, recruiting offices all over the country were besieged by volunteers eager to sign up and fight. In some places the recruiters couldn't cope and men were sent home and told to report the next day. Believe it or not there were even reports of queue jumping.

David suddenly remembered he had unfinished business with Archie and he started to poke Archie hard in the chest with his finger.

'And you! You definitely won't be alright! I don't want you going near my sister while I'm away, do you hear me?' threatened David.

'Tell him Archie, please!' Charlotte pleaded.

'I'm not speaking to him. Not until he apologises for assaulting me… and if he pokes me one more time…'

'Tell me what?' interrupted David.

'Archie's going with you, aren't you Archie, he joins up on the same day that you do.'

'Are you old chap?' asked Bertram smiling. 'Welcome to the gang, did you hear that David, he's one of us, so leave the man alone.'

David turned to Bertram and gave him a look of disdain.

'So, you needn't worry about Archie because he won't be anywhere near me, but I will be waiting for him to come home and there's nothing you can do about that brother!' said Charlotte, heatedly.

David went quiet. He was momentarily lost for words. He paced up and down whilst mulling things over. Then he suddenly stopped and turned to address Archie.

'Ok listen' began David 'If you want to carry on courting my sister you have to do the honourable thing and ask my father's permission.'

'No, he doesn't David,' protested Charlotte.

'It's ok Charlotte,' assured Archie. 'I'm willing to do that.'

David started to laugh.

'You might want to rethink your decision Archie, personally I'd rather go to war,' said Bertram.

'When?' Archie asked.

'How about tomorrow at five o'clock?' suggested David. 'I'll let my father know that we'll be having one more guest for tea.'

David offered Archie his hand and said 'let's seal the deal.' Archie shook David's hand firmly.

'Seal your fate more like,' said Charlotte, who was not happy at the turn of events.

Archie drew Charlotte to one side. 'Surely it won't be that bad?' asked Archie, who was feeling a little uneasy following Charlotte's comment.

'You haven't met my father, have you?' Charlotte replied.

'Come on Charlotte, it's time you were home, and you Butler, had better not be late tomorrow. If there's one thing my father can't stand, it's lateness!' David shouted over his shoulder as he turned to leave.

David and Bertram walked away, laughing together as they strode back down the embankment. Archie leaned over and kissed Charlotte on the cheek.

'I'll see you tomorrow then... oh and thanks for the locket.'

Charlotte hurried off to join her brother and Bertie. She looked back, smiled and waved at Archie.

Chapter 3

18th August 1914

Archie was dressed in his Sunday best and felt rather nervous as he stood outside the Manning residence. He braced himself to knock on the door, then hesitated, he suddenly had second thoughts about meeting Charlotte's father. He turned to leave but it was too late, the door opened.

'Bloody hell, you made it then. You're braver than I thought Butler, come on in,' said David. 'We've all been waiting for you.' There was a friendlier tone to David's voice when he spoke to Archie today.

Archie took off his hat as he entered the Manning's home. It was much the same as the one where he lived. A three-bedroom terraced house with an outside toilet, a front parlour, and a dining room with a scullery attached, that acted as a kitchen. Most family events happened in the dining room, it was usually the busiest room in the house. As was usual in most working-class homes of that time, the sitting room, or front parlour, was reserved for special occasions, such as birthdays and Christmas, or for special guests. Archie had assumed he would be introduced to Charlotte's parents in the sitting room, but David led him down the hallway towards the dining room.

Archie entered the dining room with a sense of trepidation. The Manning family were gathered around the dining table. Mr and Mrs Manning, their youngest son Michael, and Charlotte, who was feeling a little anxious, all looked towards him as he set foot in the room.

'You're on time young man, so that's a good start. Well, don't just stand there like a wet weekend lad, take your coat off and sit yourself down, this food won't eat its self you know,' Mr Manning said firmly.

Archie sat down in silence. On the table was a large bowl of homegrown salad, a plate of cooked meats, a bread board with a freshly baked loaf and a butter dish, lots of cakes and a large pot of tea. David took his seat at the table, next to his father. Mr Manning said grace before the family tucked into the abundant food.

'A very nice spread Mrs Manning and the cakes look delicious,' said Archie.

Mrs Manning smiled as she acknowledged his compliment. 'Thank you ducky, it's very nice of you to say so.'

'So young man,' began Mr Manning.

'My name is Archie, sir.'

'I'm quite aware of what your name is. I'll start again.'

David sniggered and was elbowed sharply by Charlotte.

'So young man. I hear you answered the call to fight for your country, just like my brave son here.' He patted David on the back.

'That's right, Mr Manning.'

'And you're joining the same regiment and reporting on the same day I believe?'

'That's right, Mr Manning.'

'Tell me lad, are you a parrot?'

'No, Mr Manning.'

'Don't forget father, I'm going with them too,' said Michael.

'Oh no you're not Michael. You're only fifteen, you have to be nineteen to sign up,' Charlotte informed him.

'Billy Jenkins is joining up next week and he's the same age as me,' protested Michael, chewing a piece of buttered bread.

'Get your elbows off the table Michael and don't speak with your mouth full. Billy Jenkins isn't joining any Army, I'll be having words with his mother,' said Mrs Manning deciding the matter.

'You'll go when your good and ready son,' said his father. 'Now, less of your chat while I'm talking.'

'They're saying that up to thirty thousand men a day are joining up, those Germans won't know what's hit them. I bet you wish you were reporting with us Mr Manning,' Archie said.

'I'm afraid I haven't got the legs for it anymore son but if I could, I would.'

'Nonsense sir, you look like a fit man, I'm sure you'd make a good Sergeant Major.'

The room fell suddenly quiet and Mrs Manning got up and walked into the kitchen.

'Father lost both his legs in the second Boer war,' David explained.

'Oh, I'm terribly sorry, sir, I… I didn't know.'

It wasn't going too well for Archie. He wished the floor would open and swallow him up. He glanced across the table at Charlotte for a little reassurance.

'But all's well Archie lad,' said Mr Manning. 'The doctor assured me they will grow back eventually, didn't he Charlotte?'

'Father, that's awful.'

Mr Manning began to laugh loudly, as did his two sons. Archie joined in, nervously. Then Mr Manning banged his fist down hard on the table.

'Right, let's get down to business shall we. David tells me you've come here today to ask permission to court my daughter Charlotte, is that right?'

'Yes, sir.'

'Sorry, speak up lad, I didn't hear you.'

Archie cleared his throat and tried again 'Yes sir. I would like to court Charlotte sir.'

Mr Manning leaned forward and looked Archie in the eye, suspiciously.

'A little bird tells me you've already been courting Charlotte for the past six months, is that true?'

'Yes, sir, I apologise for that, sir, I...'

'So why are you asking me now, she isn't in the family way is she?' Mr Manning asked directly.

'Father!' Charlotte was outraged at her father's question.

Archie stood up sharply. 'No, sir, definitely not, sir.'

'Sit down Archie,' instructed Mr Manning.

The old man leaned back in his chair and folded his arms. Archie did as he was told and sat down too.

'You see son, I have to ask you that question, it's my duty as a father you see.'

'I understand that, sir, but Charlotte and I...' began Archie before being interrupted.

'You see that cupboard over there,' said Mr Manning as he pointed to a cupboard in the corner of the room. 'That's where I keep my shotguns.'

Archie was starting to feel a little worried and began to wonder if now would be a good time to make his excuses and leave. He looked around the room for an escape route. Then Mr Manning began to laugh.

'Relax Archie, of course you can court my daughter. I know your father, Jack, he's a good man and I know your older brothers as well. Your father often speaks very highly of you. All I ask is that you treat Charlotte right and we'll get along just fine. You have my permission lad.'

Archie sighed with relief. 'Thank you, sir. Thank you very much, sir.'

Charlotte got up and walked around the table to give her father a kiss.

'Right, who's for a game of snakes and ladders?' Mr Manning asked.

The next few weeks went by quickly and the day of enlistment soon approached. By now, David and Bertram had got used to having Archie around and the three young men formed a strong friendship, although a little argumentative at times.

The night before they took their oath for King and country they all went to the local pub to enjoy their last night of freedom. They certainly weren't the only ones in the pub that night, the pub was packed with many of their friends, who were also joining up. There was a sense of celebration in the air. Many of the young men had never been out of their home town of Derby, let alone go off to fight a war in a foreign land. Archie and Charlotte sat in a quiet corner of the pub and Charlotte looked subdued.

'You can go and join your friends Archie if you like. I'll be alright,' said Charlotte.

'I'd much rather sit here with you Charlotte, and anyway, I'm going to be spending a lot of my time with that lot,' replied Archie with a smile.

'You will write to me Archie, won't you? I want to know everything.'

'Of course I'll write to you. I'll write whenever I get the chance, it will be like you're right there with me, I promise. I won't be able to put certain things in my letters though, you know, about where I am, and what I'm up to!'

Charlotte looked shocked when he said this.

'I'm hoping you won't be up to anything Archibald Butler!'

'No, I mean my movements, military things you know, just in case the letters don't make it and fall into the wrong hands and all that, we don't want the Germans to know what we're up to do we?'

'I know Archie, I was only pulling your leg and as far as me being right there with you, I'll always be with you. I'm in that locket around your neck. You'll never take it off will you Archie? Please promise me,' begged Charlotte, as they moved closer to each other.

'Come on sis, leave the poor lad alone, it's his last night of freedom. I believe it's your round, Archie,' said David.

'Go on Archie, go and enjoy yourself. I'll be ok for a while,' said Charlotte.

The evening went well, full of high spirits and lots of singing, the atmosphere crackled with excitement at the prospect of what lay ahead. Charlotte remained seated in the corner, feeling sad and worried at the thought of what might happen to her Archie.

However, she put on a brave face and joined in with the revelry.

The church bell rang out to signify midnight. Archie was a little drunk but determined to walk his sweetheart home.

'How much have you had to drink, are you sure you don't want *me* to take you home Archie?' said Charlotte giggling.

'No, I won't have you walking home on your own Charlotte. I don't want your father reaching for that shotgun.'

'Father will be in bed by now, and anyway he wasn't telling the truth about the guns.'

They both walked past Parker's Piece and the spot where they had both lay together in the grass a few weeks earlier. Charlotte stopped and pulled Archie towards her.

'I don't want to go home just yet Archie. I want to spend the rest of the night with you.'

'But Charlotte, what about David and Bertie?'

'Did you see them? They were in no fit state to worry about anybody… please Archie.'

That night, under the stars, in the long grass, they made love for the first time and then fell asleep in each other's arms. At around five in the morning Charlotte was woken up by the sound of the birds chirping, announcing the onset of dawn.

Charlotte began to panic, 'Archie, wake up we need to get home, it's getting light.'

Archie woke quickly, the sound of alarm in her voice brought him fully awake. He jumped up and brushed himself down before offering Charlotte his arm. They hurriedly walked the short distance from the field to Charlotte's house just before the dawn broke.

'Will I be seeing you tomorrow Archie, before you go? I could take the day off work, I'll tell them I'm ill or something.' Before Charlotte could say another word, Archie put his hand up over her mouth gently.

'It's best if we don't meet tomorrow Charlotte, let's say our goodbyes now shall we. I'll only be stationed a few miles away, at Normanton Barracks. I've been told that after a few weeks of basic training we'll get a night off so don't look so sad. I promise I'll write straight away, on my first day.'

Charlotte just smiled because she was lost for words.

'Goodnight Charlotte.'

Charlotte started to cry and reached for her handkerchief.

'Don't cry, I'm sure I won't be away for long, it'll be over sooner than you think.'

'Alright Archie, I'll see you soon. I'll miss you.'

They embraced and kissed for the last time before parting.

Archie stood and waited until Charlotte was safely inside her home. He gave her a final wave as she closed the door. Her mother, who had waited up for her return, also waved from the bedroom window.

Chapter 4

Normanton Barracks opened on the 1st December 1877, and was initially the headquarters for the 54th and 95th Regiments, who later became known as the Sherwood Foresters. During the Boer War and World War One it was an important training and deployment depot. Nearly all of the men who enlisted in the Regiment were from the counties of Nottinghamshire and Derbyshire. During the War, the Regiment expanded to thirty-three Battalions. War was declared against Germany on the 4th August 1914 at eleven o'clock that evening. The British Army was not prepared for the number of volunteers who came forward in those first few months.

Archie, David and Bertram joined the newly formed 10th Battalion of the Sherwood Foresters. Happy and excited about what the day may hold, they said goodbye to their families and travelled together to the barracks, arriving early. It was just after nine o'clock when they arrived at the barracks but their actual reporting time was at ten o'clock.

'Wait over there, you'll be escorted to where you need to be when the rest arrive,' said a guard commander, who then disappeared back inside his guardroom to be reunited with his cup of tea.

'It looks like we're the only three joining up,' David said, noticing a distinct lack of other men.

'That's good, I hate crowded places. Eh, you don't think the others have had second thoughts do you?' asked Bertram.

The three young men weren't on their own for long. Within half an hour, it went from three to three hundred, there were volunteers everywhere. It seemed like everybody knew somebody, old friends from school or from work, family friends and cousins, which in some way, made the men feel at home. From there they were all escorted to a large hall, where they were informed about the events of the next few days, should they make it that far. They were told that they would have to undertake fitness, medical and eye tests, carried out by medical examiners, but before all of that, all new recruits were required to show proof of age.

'Come on you lot, form an orderly queue!' barked the training Sergeant, whose name was Sergeant Shirley, a rather fat and unfit looking man, who must have been in his late fifties.

Bertram, David and Archie, joined the growing line of men. The air buzzed with excitement, as though the men in the queue were heading off for a day at the seaside, not preparing to go to war.

'What an unhealthy, ugly bunch we have here, how the hell you cretins are going to pass your medicals I can't imagine. Christ knows what the enemy will think when they see you lot coming. Right gentlemen, start stripping off, leaving your undergarments on, we don't want to see your dangly bits do we. Come on, move it, I haven't got all day, nor has the British army, there's a war on you know God help us,' Sergeant Shirley shouted.

To pass the medical at the outbreak of World War One, you had to be the right height and weight and be sufficiently intelligent. Your eye sight was expected to be up to the required standard. You were also expected to have good hearing, speech without impediment, no glandular swellings, chest capacious and well formed, heart and lungs to be sound, limbs well formed and fully developed, free and perfect motion of all the joints, feet and toes well formed, no congenital malformation or defects, not bear traces of previous acute or chronic diseases and in the possession of a sufficient number of sound teeth.

David and Archie had completed their medical and were passed fit. Now it was Bertram's turn to go in front of the medical examiner. Everything was going well until it came to the procedure that all new recruits dreaded, the examination of the scrotum to see if the testicles were descended and normal.

'Ok drop them private,' said the medical examiner.

Bertram didn't move and looked a little unsure.

'Come on, don't be shy what's up with you man, I haven't got all day. I need to examine your trunk. Stand with your arms extended above your head please. What is it man? Spit it out.'

'Sir, I just want to say something before I do this, there has to be an element of trust here.'

'What are you talking about man?'

The Sergeant realised that the queue of recruits being examined had slowed down and so he wandered over to see what the problem was.

'Problem sir?' Sergeant Shirley asked the examiner.

'Yes, Sergeant, can you tell this man that we're all men here, and if he doesn't complete the medical he won't be able to join up.'

'That's ok, I'll be off then,' said Bertram as he started to walk away.

'Get back here you.' Sergeant Shirley was not amused.

'Excuse me, you can't talk to me like that,' said Bertram.

'Shut up!' The Sergeant addressed Bertram by talking close to his ear. 'What's your name?'

'Bertram.'

'Your surname you cretin, and it's Sergeant to you.'

'Ward, Sergeant.'

'Right Ward, drop them for the medical examiner there's a good lad.'

Reluctantly Bertram complied while everyone looked on, there was some sniggering from those standing nearby.

'Oh dear, not very well made are we?'

'With all respect Sergeant we're only fighting the Germans, aren't we?'

Everyone started to laugh at Bertram's reply.

'Silence you lot... so you think you're a comedian do you Ward? Come and see me later. I have a little job for you, we'll see who has the last laugh.'

Once they had passed the various tests the men were given lunch, their first army meal and then they marched back to the hall to make a solemn promise to do their duty.

The ceremony was led by the recruiting officers. New soldiers swore an oath of allegiance to the King upon a Bible. The oath required every new recruit to swear to 'faithfully defend His Majesty, His Heirs and successors...against all enemies'. Also thrown in for good measure, each man was required to promise to obey the authority of 'all Generals and Officers set over them'. Lastly, all recruits had to pledge to serve as long as the war lasted. They all now belonged to the British army and from that moment everything changed.

The men were split into groups of twenty-four and marched to the stores to collect their bedding and temporary uniforms. From there they made their way to their new temporary accommodation, a large brick building consisting of four, twenty-four man rooms, two on the ground floor and two on the first floor, with a central staircase and central latrines on each floor, along with a few smaller rooms.

It had been a long day so far. Thankfully, once they'd been allocated a bed space, shown around their new living quarters and had listened to a briefing about the next day's events, the rest of that day was theirs.

Archie and David were trying out their new beds.

'Not bad, not as good as my bed at home, but I've slept on worse and that dinner wasn't too bad either.' David said.

'So, this is it, we are soldiers now, how does that make you feel David?' Archie asked.

'I'll let you know in a few days,' David replied, lying flat on his back puffing away on a cigarette.

'Is that when we plan our escape?' Bertram asked.

'Talking of escape Bertie… here comes your new best friend, fat Sergeant Shirley.' Archie had spotted the Sergeant striding through the door.

'Oh bugger.'

'Private Ward, I've been looking for you,' Sergeant Shirley said, before informing Bertram of his punishment.

After speaking to Bertram, the Sergeant told everyone to make their way to the cook-house for tea. By five o'clock the men were all back in their billets, apart from Bertram, who had been instructed to stay behind. He'd been put on cook-house fatigues as punishment, washing and drying pans and peeling spuds for the next day's dinner. It was almost eight o'clock before Bertram returned to his billet and although he was tired he was determined to record the day's events in his diary.

Dear Diary,

My first day. The day started well until I was bawled at by this rather arrogant, short, fat Sergeant who, after giving us what for, ordered us all to strip off for the medical. I can't believe I've been put on cook-house fatigues for not dropping my undergarments quick enough. But nothing could have prepared me for what came next. The most embarrassing part of the whole medical was when the medical examiner examined my scrotum to see if the testicles were descended and normal.

He didn't have to do what he did? I could have told him they were correct. I can't explain what he did, but it was most uncomfortable. But spare a thought for the handful of lads that failed the medical for a variety of reasons, wrong height, wrong weight, bad eyesight, bad heart, TB, syphilis, to name but a few. Training starts tomorrow, I can't wait to start, but I feel I might end up regretting those words. And when the training is over I look forward to embarking on this adventure of a lifetime. Well, that's what they told me when I signed up for this war.

Archie had made good his promise to write to Charlotte about his first day. He had spent some time composing his letter in his head before committing it to paper.

My Dearest Charlotte,

I know I'm only a short distance away, but I did promise I'd write to you straight away. I hope you don't mind. Well, my love, I am now a soldier in the King's army and feel very proud. We all passed the medical with flying colours, even Bertram!

They are saying we will be here for two weeks before we leave to do our basic training. We will find out tomorrow where we'll be going, I hope it's not too far away. In the mean time we'll just be doing some initial training, we start tomorrow morning at six o'clock.

Today we were given a strange blue uniform and cardboard cap badges. We were the lucky ones, some of the lads didn't even get a uniform. They told us we'll get our proper uniforms soon and a rifle. It wouldn't surprise me if the rifles were made of cardboard too. It's understandable really with the number of troops here, it's overwhelming.

We are lucky to be billeted in the barracks. It's that full here some of the men have been billeted in the surrounding church halls, schools and warehouses.

Sorry I have to stop writing now, it's lights out in ten minutes. I wonder what tomorrow will bring. I will write again soon.

Your loving soldier

Archie xxx

Whilst stationed at Normanton Barracks the men were allowed to book out at the guardroom after tea and visit their loved ones, but they all had to be back in their billets before lights out. It took a few days for the men to adapt to the routine of army life. Bertram continued to keep a record of events.

Dear Diary,

Our day starts at five-thirty when the bugler calls reveille to wake us all up. After a quick tidy up of the room we grab a brew before fitness training at six-thirty. Wash, shave then breakfast at eight-thirty, and then we spend all morning drilling on the parade square. Twelve-thirty lunch, before returning for more fitness training and you've guessed it, more bloody drill until four-fifteen.

If you are the unlucky one or your drill isn't up to the required standard or you have a Sergeant that has it in for you, you might be detailed off for fatigues or work parties. I've just about had my fill of fitness and drill and fatigues. When is the real training going to begin?

Returning from the cook house on their fifth day of training, the three friends relaxed until lights out. As yet, none of them had taken the opportunity to visit their loved ones.

'I wonder what the German training is like? I can't wait to get over there, and out drill them!!! So far that's all we know how to do, oh and running, we are now trained in running,' said Bertram, lying on his bed.

'At least we'll be able to outrun them if things get a bit scary out there, eh Bertie,' Archie replied.

Chapter 5

After some basic training close to home, the 10th Battalion moved to Wool in Dorset. The recruits were put under the command of a regular officer of the Sherwood Foresters called Captain Stackhouse, an officer of high standing and a leader of men.

All new recruits underwent months of basic training in various camps dotted all over the country, where they were turned into soldiers and the new officers learned to lead their men. Inside these camps the transformation from civilians to soldiers began and they said goodbye to their old lives.

The men arrived at Wool expecting to be wearing khaki or at the very least be able to lay their hands on a weapon of some description, but there was nothing. Not only did the majority of men have no uniform or weapon, there were no food rations for them either. However, the morale of the men was still good, but they were hungry after the journey from the Midlands.

'What are we supposed to eat? It didn't take long for things to start going downhill,' Bertram said, shaking his head.

'We can't carry on like this, no proper uniforms, no rifles and now no food,' Archie replied.

'And we're still in bloody Blighty. What will it be like when we move over there?' said one of the men who was standing nearby.

The Captain who had broken the news to the men that the rations hadn't arrived, ordered them to go into the woods and villages to forage for food and so that is what they did.

'I can't believe it. What sort of army is this? An army marches on its stomach doesn't it? That's what I've always been told, they didn't tell us we had to chase our dinner around the woods,' said Bertram.

'Come on, we'd best start foraging hadn't we, before there's bugger all left,' replied David.

It wasn't long before the local countryside was crawling with men all looking for something to eat, nothing edible was safe. Archie and David descended on one local farm, while Bertram tried his luck at another. After explaining their situation, the farmer gave them a dozen eggs, a large bag of apples and a large loaf of freshly baked bread. They all returned to camp that night happy with their prizes, including Bertram, who returned with the biggest prize of all, a small pig, which he walked into camp on a piece of string.

'Bertram you are a hero, you have a pig!' exclaimed one of the other soldiers.

'Yes, I exchanged him for my spare pocket watch. I've decided to call him Shirley after that fat training Sergeant at Normanton Barracks.'

'That's a kind gesture Bertie. I'm sure he would love that,' Archie replied.

'It looks like we're feasting tonight boys, Shirley will feed us all,' David said.

'What! Oh no, I don't want to kill him,' Bertram answered, with a note of fear in his voice.

'What are you going to do with him then?' Archie asked.

'I've grown quite fond of Shirley now.' Bertram picked up his new friend and cradled him, reluctant to let him go.

'I'm sorry Bertie old mate, the pig will have to go,' David insisted. 'A pet pig won't be much use where we're going old chap.'

Bertram looked down at his new friend with sad eyes and reluctantly agreed.

'Ok, if you must, but I refuse to be responsible for Shirley's murder.'

'It will be painless Bertram,' Archie assured him.

'Well, who's doing the deadly deed? Any volunteers?' Bertram asked.

The men just sat looking at each other, nobody appeared to want to be responsible for dispatching the pig. Then David took out his knife, picked up Shirley and walked into the nearby woods, out of sight. A few minutes later they all heard a squeal. Shirley was no more. David soon arrived back with the dead pig.

'Bloody hell look at all your glum faces. It's only a pig, if you have a problem killing a bloody pig what are you going to be like over there?'

David had thrown his marker down and from then on, he was regarded as someone not to be messed with. 'Right, get that fire going.'

That night they sat around campfires and feasted. It seemed to them to be an amusing way to spend their first night at training camp. Tomorrow, the real training would begin.

The next morning the new Quarter Master arrived at the camp. A Lieutenant, S.J. Pearsall, whose nickname was 'Willie.' From that day forward there was always rations forthcoming for the men. Soon other officers arrived and took up their posts, first the Adjutant, and then the Company Commanders.

Archie, Bertram and David were now part of C Company, commanded by a Major Moran. The officer that stood out most of all was the new second in command, Major J.C. Keown, who arrived wearing a bowler hat and carrying an umbrella. The men sat around watching the comings and goings.

'Look at him,' said Archie, 'he looks like a detective.'

'The case of the murdered pig… Who killed Shirley?' Everyone started to laugh at David's reply.

'You're not funny, we all know who the murderer was, don't we David? I liked that pig.' Bertram still hadn't forgiven David.

'So did my stomach!' David answered.

The small group of officers had a mammoth task ahead of them and only a short time to complete it. The men were divided into companies and platoons and the job of the officers was to knock the men into shape, until they resembled a battalion of soldiers to be proud of, and this they did. It was said by some of the surviving members of the battalion, that the Commanding Officer, Captain Stackhouse, achieved this with an iron hand and the men respected him for it.

Captain Stackhouse's job was done and he returned to the first Battalion. He was replaced by Lieutenant Colonel W E Banbury of the Indian army, who took over the 10th Battalion. Sadly, Captain Stackhouse was later killed at Neuve Chapelle.

Bertram continued to write in his diary, although the entries became intermittent.

20th December 1914

Dear Diary,

We are now part of the 51st Infantry Brigade, 17th Division so I've been informed, whatever that means! It seems like new officers are joining us on a daily basis.

Today we were introduced to our new section commander and he's an odd chap. Rumour has it he wanted to be an officer but didn't make the grade, so they made him a Corporal. I have heard Corporal Robinson was an accountant before he joined up, this is evident in the way he has to record every small detail in a notebook he carries with him.

The weather has been damn wretched since we got here, we are still living in tents which are made from very inadequate canvas, one would be dryer sleeping outside. There is icy mud everywhere, even inside the tents, sometimes it is two inches high. The tent pegs lose their hold all the time, causing the tents to collapse. Blankets, bedding, clothes and the men end up plastered with mud. If these conditions keep up it could have an effect on our health and morale.

We heard one of the other regiments organised a strike against the weather conditions, this movement met with no encouragement from the 10th.

Would you believe it, we actually have an officer in charge of drains, a Lieutenant Giles! Drains are being dug continually, zigzagging in every direction, we navigate from tent to tent using old duckboards, there are large holes everywhere. I fear if I slip I will disappear never to be seen again down one of these chasms. One of the lads saw a rat this morning, I hope this isn't a sign of things to come.

We all enjoy the training so far, although it's getting a little repetitive with virtually no equipment. If we are not running around the countryside, we are doing drill or bayonet practice which is easy and great fun, all we have to do is run at sacks full of straw screaming our heads off. Even I can do that. I'm sure the sacks will be easy to outwit in a battle situation!!

Bertram didn't have to wait too long. The training was about to change from basic to more advanced. It began with learning field craft (the basics of movement in the field) then they were introduced to night operations and route marching. Later, when some rifles arrived, it was weapons handling, marksmanship and learning how to dig proper trenches and living in them. The average working day was around ten hours.

Chapter 6

23th December 1914

Training had been cancelled due to the bad weather and the men lay in their leaky tents. There were men from every walk of life, bank clerks and teachers, factory workers and shop workers, all crammed together, some were sleeping, some writing home and others were just day dreaming of home. For many of these men it was their first time away from home and many of them quickly became homesick.

Bertram paused from reading his bible to listen to the heavy rain hitting the canvas.

'I do wish this rain would stop,' he said.

'Maybe it's time to think about building that ark, Bertie. Doesn't it warn you in that book of yours?' David joked.

'That would be Genesis, chapter seven. The Lord said to Noah, 'Go into the ark, you and your whole family, because I have found you righteous in this generation. Take with you seven pairs of every kind of clean animal, a male and its mate, and one pair of every kind of unclean animal, a male and his mate…'

'Ok Bertram that's enough. The only animals you get around here are rats and possibly plenty of ducks and fish, if this water gets any deeper,' said David.

Archie was busy reading a recent letter from Charlotte and he looked on edge.

'Are you ok Archie, you look a bit worried, everything good at home?' David asked.

'Yes, I'm fine, everybody is well and sends their love.'

But Archie wasn't fine, he was far from it. He reread the contents of the letter hoping he had misread it.

My Dearest Archie,

I hope this letter finds you in good health. Archie, I have something to tell you, I'm hoping you react to what I'm going to say with calmness. I am with child Archie. The only person I've told so far is mother and now you.

I don't know whether to be happy or sad at this news. I only found out the other day. What is my father going to say, what is David going to say or more importantly what are you going to say?

Archie read on, holding the locket he wore around his neck, his mind full of mixed emotions. He felt both happy and sad by the sudden news. He wished he could be with her. Archie was fearful of the consequences to come so he had to pick the right time to tell Charlotte's brother, David. He's going to kill me, he thought.

There was no leave that Christmas, but the men were given the day off on Christmas day. Christmas dinner was good, under the circumstances, and there was a plentiful supply of rum and beer for the men

to drown their sorrow at not being able to go home
and be amongst their family, friends and loved ones.

Early in the New Year their living conditions
improved. Huts were slowly erected for the men,
while the officers still had to battle with the
elements, remaining under canvas in a nearby pine
wood.

By February, the Royal Engineers had arrived and
set about digging the new ranges. At last, a number
of short rifles arrived and the men got the chance to
fire musketry for the first time. Training was an
immense challenge in the First World War. Time,
space, kit and experienced instructors were all in
short supply during the onset of the war.

One evening, after visiting the new rifle ranges,
Archie and Bertram were busy cleaning their rifles in
their hut and Archie decided to tell Bertram about
Charlotte's pregnancy. David was on another range
detail and hadn't arrived back yet. Bertie looked
shocked at first when Archie told him the news, but
then he started to laugh.

'It's not funny Bertie,' Archie said.

'Not funny for you but funny for me. What were
you thinking Archie? Obviously you weren't thinking
at all. David won't be happy you know, and as far as
Mr Manning is concerned, well, you'll be better off
taking your chances in France rather than go home
right now.'

'Thanks, I was hoping for support and some
sensible advice Bertie.'

'Advice… my advice is to start running Archie and don't stop.'

'I was thinking of telling the Platoon Commander.'

'Platoon Commander, what's he going to do? He's even younger than you,' replied Bertram.

The young officers had to be taught how to command and take care of the men under their control. The platoon commanders were mostly junior officers or second lieutenants, some of whom were just teenagers, who couldn't even take care of themselves. Each officer was in command of a platoon of around thirty men, many of whom were from tougher and rougher backgrounds than the officers in charge. If a young officer didn't get it right the men soon let them know about it.

'If you want my advice,' said Bertie 'Firstly, I wouldn't tell David just yet, pick your moment. He'll be back from the ranges shortly, with his rifle still in his possession, so that would be bad timing. Secondly, do you love the girl?'

'Yes, I do, dearly,' said Archie earnestly.

'Then you need to wed the girl as soon as possible. Write to her father and ask him if you can marry his daughter, he most probably knows about it by now and is expecting you to do exactly that with all haste. Once her father knows it won't be long before David gets wind of it. Leave David to me. I'll tell him tonight,' said Bertie.

That evening, after tea, they all lay on their beds relaxing. Archie looked like a man who was about to have all his teeth pulled out. He knew what was coming, so he left the billet to breathe some fresh air. As soon as Archie went outside, Bertram got off his own bed and sat down on the end of David's. David lowered his week-old newspaper and looked inquisitively at Bertram before lifting his newspaper up to his face again.

'What is it Bertie? I know you're dying to tell me something, it's written all over your ugly face, come on man, spit it out.'

After a long pause, Bertram drew a deep breath and gave David the news.

'It's your sister Charlotte.'

'What about Charlotte?'

'She's pregnant.'

David didn't react immediately but his mind quickly worked out the scenario.

'Where is he?'

'Calm down David.'

'Where is he! I'm going to fucking kill him. So, he didn't have the balls to tell me himself. Well he certainly won't have any balls left when I've finished with him!'

'Calm down David, it's not the end of the world. You're going to be an Uncle,' Bertram said, which made David even angrier.

David began walking up and down the billet and his anger towards Archie intensified with every step he took.

'I warned him! What did I say?! Now look what's gone and happened! He just couldn't keep it in his bloody trousers could he! Bloody hell, what an embarrassing mess. God knows what my father will say! Maybe I should just strangle him and tell everyone he copped for it in France.'

'I suppose that's a plan' said Bertram.

David pushed Bertram out of his way and headed for the latrines. Bertram hurried after him, along with half of the platoon who were eager to witness what the outcome was going to be.

'Come on out Archie, I know you're in there! Come out now or I'll be knocking that door down!' shouted David as he hammered on the latrine door with his fist.

Archie opened the door to face his punishment, smiling as though it wasn't a big deal, trying to play down the situation.

'You wanted to speak to me David?'

He closed his eyes and waited for the impact of David's fist. The Platoon looked on and some of the men laughed at Archie's predicament. David turned to face them, his anger clearly evident.

'What are you all staring at, fuck off back to your hut, there's nothing to see here, go on, move it!'

The Platoon members retreated slowly, not wanting David to turn on them in his angry state.

'I'm sorry David, it's come as a shock to me… it really has,' Archie said, in a quavering voice.

David grabbed Archie by the scruff of his neck.

'So, what are you trying to tell me Archie, that you're not the father is that what you're telling me eh… eh?'

'No David, it must have been that night I was drunk, the night before we joined up.'

'Be careful old chap, you're strangling him,' cautioned Bertram.

'Strangle him, I'll do more than strangle him. What am I to do with you eh, you're too young to shoot and too skinny for my bayonet. Right, you're coming with me, come on,' David instructed, as he grabbed Archie's arm.

'Where are we going?' Archie asked, fearing the worst.

'He's probably going to take you into the wood where he took my Shirley,' Bertram answered.

A wave of relief washed over Archie as David dragged him towards the padre's accommodation and not the woods. A while later, after speaking to the padre, both men stood in front of the Company Commander, along with their Platoon Sergeant, Sergeant Johnson. After explaining the situation, David requested compassionate leave, so that Archie could do the decent thing and marry his sister.

'Hmm, what do you think Sergeant?' asked the Company Commander.

'What do I think, sir? I think he should face the firing squad sir. If that was my daughter, I'd make sure of it, however, we need every man we can get.'

'Have you any children Sergeant?'

'Six, sir, and they all drive me crazy, so I think he should face up to his responsibilities and marry the girl.'

'Ok, I'm granting you both forty-eight hours leave. Private Manning, this man is now your prisoner, make sure he goes home and does the honourable thing by marrying the girl. Now get out of my sight before I change my mind.'

David and Archie were issued with travel warrants for their journey home. They arrived to a cold family atmosphere but the initial bitterness in the air soon mellowed. The wedding was hastily arranged, as were so many other weddings during the Great War. The following day, Archie and Charlotte were married. The wedding celebration that evening was a joyous affair and all the ill feelings were soon forgotten. Now young Archie had a wife and he was going to be a father, but he also had a war to take care of. How things had changed for young Archie in such a short time, this young man had come of age pretty quickly.

In early April, the weather had improved and the battalion was on the move again, to a canvas camp close to Lulworth, where they spent the whole of that spring. It was a picturesque place and the local woods were alive with primroses and bluebells. On hot afternoons, the battalion was allowed to bathe on the beaches at Durdle Door.

It wasn't long before the real training began, to prepare them for what was to come. Soon, those happy, healthy days had gone, resigned to memory. Sadly, many of those young men would never experience them again.

The training was intended to be as realistic as possible and to emulate the real live conditions of war. On one particular day, the battalion marched ten miles in full kit, to relieve a battalion of the 50th Brigade, who were positioned in training trenches in Wareham. They then spent the day learning all about trench warfare and enacting war games. During the night, they were relieved by another Battalion and marched back to camp, arriving at dawn the next day.

Dear Diary,

The lie factory is in full flow, rumours and more rumours, to be quite honest, these rumours about the date of our crossing to France are an inexhaustible topic of conversation and the date is always in two months. Now we've been told the division has been selected for Home Defence duties, so apparently, we won't be going to France after all. I've decided to ignore all rumours from now on. They are sending me slowly mad.

On the 16th May, Archie received the news that Charlotte had given birth to a baby boy, Archie junior. The first person to congratulate him was

David, who, from nowhere produced a crate of ale and a large bottle of rum.

'Where did you get this from?' Archie asked.

'We've been saving up haven't we lads?' replied David, indicating their fellow hut mates.

'Congratulations brother-in-law. Well, what are we waiting for? It's time to wet the baby's head.'

That night the drinking went on until the early hours. The bond between the three men was now very strong, especially when Archie asked Bertram to be Godfather to his baby son.

At the end of May the Division was on the move again, they were off to Winchester, but this time it was different. They had to march for five consecutive days and bivouac each night. Luckily the weather was good and some of the countryside was delightful. On 30th of May they arrived at Flowerdown Camp, near Winchester.

This was to be the last posting for the 10th Battalion before they left for France. Very little training was carried out during this posting, due to the dense countryside, so a system of trenches was dug by the Royal Engineers, so that the battalion could train for trench warfare.

The men were excited when the short Lee Enfield rifles arrived, at long last they sensed that something was happening. The men finally had real rifles, up until now, ninety percent of the rifles they'd been using were for drill purposes only. From that day on they were constantly out on the ranges and a large amount of musketry was fired. The soldiers also had a few days of field firing. More and more equipment began to arrive, including Lewis guns and signalling equipment.

On the 10th July, Archie, David and Bertram were sitting outside the billet, cleaning their rifles, when they heard the news.

'Right, listen in you lot, it's official, no more rumours. We move overseas on the 14th' announced the Platoon Sergeant, Sergeant Johnson. The news was met with huge excitement, the waiting was over and all the men cheered.

'I suppose that's you done then Sergeant, you'll be going home to your six kids,' Bertram said.

The men had always assumed that Sergeant Johnson had been drafted in solely for the training of the recruits and that he was too old to go off to fight a war.

'No lad, I'll be on that boat with you, you can be sure about that.'

The men were happy to hear that he was going to be with them. Despite his grumpiness at times, Sergeant Johnson had become something of a father figure to his men.

'I might have a wife and six kids at home, but I've got thirty big kids to look after here,' remarked Sergeant Johnson and then continued to address the men. 'As we speak, lots are being drawn to decide which of you lucky men will be granted forty-eight hours leave. The list of names will be put up in the orderly room at fourteen hundred hours, good luck.'

'I bet I'm not one of the lucky ones. I've never been lucky me,' complained Bertram.

'You never know Bertie,' replied David 'It might be your lucky day. I know it won't be me or Archie, we've had our quota of leave.'

Archie's heart sank at the prospect of not being able to see his baby son or wife.

'I'd love to see Charlotte and my new baby son before we depart. I'm afraid that I may never see them again.'

'Eh, we'll have none of that sort of talk! You'll be coming back, you can be sure of that, we'll all be coming back,' said David, with conviction.

'If David says we're coming back, then we're coming back,' Bertram added.

'Anyway, I've got Charlotte with me at all times, right here in my locket and when I have a picture of Archie junior he'll be in there as well.'

The lots were drawn and the lucky few prepared to go on leave. As expected, Archie, David and Bertie were not amongst the fortunate ones. This outcome didn't go down too well with the other men and before long the whole battalion descended on the orderly room demanding the same forty-eight hour leave. After some deliberation, this leave was granted to every man.

The officers and men went off in two batches, to spend some precious time with their loved ones. Archie would see his new baby boy after all. For most, this leave would be their last. Surprisingly, there wasn't one absentee when reporting back.

Chapter 7

14th July 1915

The battalion paraded to board the trains which departed for Folkestone, via Southampton. Once on board ship, the men were waved off by patriotic civilians as they set sail to Boulogne in France. Most of the men had never been on a boat before. Every soldier was given a pay book, along with a message from Lord Kitchener, reminding them to be 'courteous, considerate and kind' to the locals and allied soldiers, and an unlikely request to 'avoid the temptations of wine and women.'

They docked the next morning and marched to a camp called St Martins, situated on a hill near the town. They rested and ate a meal there before they moved on again. Soon, these men would engage in one of the deadliest, most gruelling human conflicts in history. After their meal the men had to send home their first Service postcards to inform their loved ones they had arrived safely. It was mandatory.

'I must say these postcard things are delightful, don't you think? A sort of lazy man's letter, even you can write home now David' Bertram said.

'You can keep your bloody lazy man's letter writing, all that malarkey is not for me thanks, and anyway what is there to write about yet?' David replied.

'Why do we need all this bloody equipment, a few months ago we didn't have enough, now we have too much. The Infantry man is just something to hang things on,' complained Bertram.

That afternoon the Battalion were back on the march, heading for Pont de Briques Station. Many of the men insisted on marching on the left side of the road, which they were accustomed to doing.

'Get over to your right, you lot, this is France remember!' shouted Sergeant Johnson.

'Aren't we supposed to be marching on the other side of the road?' Archie asked, confused by the order.

'No Archie, here in France they drive on the right, in fact they do everything differently here, they even eat frogs and horses,' informed Bertram.

'Horses? That's disgusting!' Archie grimaced as he spoke.

'They also eat privates, if they find any squashed in the road by oncoming horse drawn guns. Now get in file!' the Platoon Sergeant ordered. 'Sort your men out Corporal Robinson.'

The platoon had to move off the road completely to allow an endless stream of fully laden supply wagons to go past on one side of the road and the returning empty wagons to go by on the other.

They reached the station, boarded the train and headed for St. Omer, arriving there around midnight. The men then marched through the night to their billet in Zudausques. During the march they stopped at the roadside for a short smoking break.

'I don't know about you, but I'm fucked,' exclaimed David, 'my feet are killing me.'

'Watch your swearing David,' Archie reminded him.

'Watch my swearing? I can fucking swear when I want.'

'You'll be in big trouble if the Platoon Commander hears you. You heard him say that any man will be severely punished if he hears them using bad language of any kind. He said the only time that one is allowed to use bad language is in the heat of battle. In other words, if the swearing is directed at the Hun, while they are trying to kill you,' said Corporal Robinson.

'Well, my feet are trying to fucking kill me so I'm directing my obscenities at those,' retorted David.

'Shush, can you hear that?' said one of the men.

Dawn was breaking and for the first time they could hear the muffled sound of gunfire coming from miles away in the distance.

'Wow! Isn't that something, I can't wait to get amongst it all,' said Archie excitedly.

'From the sound of that I'd rather be sitting and watching it all from a safe distance thanks,' Bertram replied.

The battalion spent two days in Zudausques before moving on once again, to a village called Caestre. The march was a tough one. The heat of the day and the paved roads didn't help, marching was difficult. The closer they got to Caestre the sound of the constant gunfire became louder and louder. On a clear evening the gunfire lit up the sky and the noise of it rumbled like an approaching storm that never arrived. Another sign that they were getting close to the front was the amount of discarded German ammunition boxes abandoned by the side of the road, where the Germans had been pushed back.

Apart from the routine inspections, the battalion did very little during their week at Caestre, just resting mostly… and waiting. Archie spent some of his time writing a letter to his young wife.

My Dearest Charlotte,

While I sit writing you this letter it seems strange we are so near the front. This country is so peaceful looking, it is hard to believe that the fighting is so close. To walk across the fields is just like taking a stroll over Parker's Piece on a quiet Sunday afternoon. But the big guns are out there, we can hear them constantly now, they are not so many miles away.

This morning we had the best breakfast since landing here. We had fried eggs, bacon and tomatoes, tea, butter, strawberry jam, and bread. The bread was white bread too, I only wish I could have a breakfast like it every morning.

Well, I must close now. So goodbye to you my dearest Charlotte, you and little Archie are always uppermost in my thoughts you both mean the world to me.

Your loving husband,

Archie xxx

It was an anxious time for the men who spent so much time just waiting to move forward to the front line and it frayed the nerves of many of them. Some soldiers were eager to fight for their king and country, but others began to truly fear the thought of what was to come.

'Are we ever going to join this damn war? All it seems to be is hurry up and wait, we've now spent a whole week doing bugger all apart from taking part in these senseless inspections to keep the hierarchy happy,' complained Archie.

'Don't worry your chance will come soon enough' David replied.

It wasn't long before Archie got his wish. On the 25th of July, the Battalion was destined for the infamous Salient, where they would experience real trench warfare for the first time. They marched at night it wasn't long before they could clearly see the lights on the front line. The men sang as they marched up the road, pumped full of courage and eager for the fight. The singing faltered when they saw the returning lorries on the other side of the road, all loaded with wounded soldiers, huddled together. Their faces told a thousand stories.

A message came down the line from a sensitive officer up front. 'No smoking and no singing – pass it on.'

When they arrived at the Salient, each company was sent to a different location for their tour of instruction. A Company was sent to Sanctuary Wood, held by the 7th Battalion Sherwood Foresters. B and C Companies went for instruction in the trenches held by 52nd Brigade, near St Eloi. After twenty-four hours, the Battalion felt it was a complete waste of time because it became clear that the instructors knew little more about trench warfare than the men they were supposed to be instructing.

On the night of the 15th August, the men saw action for the first time when they relieved the 7th East Yorkshires in trenches immediately south of Ypres, at a place called Comines canal.

At Ypres, the ground was very boggy and the water table very high, making it impossible to dig a proper trench, so the trenches were built up using sandbags and wood for support. They moved into the trenches under darkness, took up their positions and looked out at No Man's Land. It was pitch black until a star shell was flung up between the trenches and flooded the whole area with light. Various types of illuminating projectile were used on the front. Rockets carrying parachutes, light ball shells, which blazed furiously for about a minute and light ball cartridges shot from a specific pistol.

The only poor souls out in No Man's Land were either dead, dying or from a listening patrol. These patrols were hazardous to say the very least. Their only chance of survival if a light went up, would be to fling themselves on the ground immediately and remain still.

The lads lay in their firing positions waiting for first light, this was it, they'd trained hard for this moment. Dawn was the most likely time for an enemy attack, soldiers were woken up and sent to their stand-to positions to guard their frontline.

'Quiet here isn't it', remarked Bertram.

'Just how I like it, I love this light show,' David replied.

David glanced at his brother-in-law and looked concerned.

'Are you shaking Archie, you're not scared, are you?'

'No… well a little,' Archie answered.

'If my sister could see her hero now,' said David, shaking his head.

'Nothing wrong with being scared Archie, it keeps you alert, and for your information I'm scared too,' Bertram said.

It wasn't quiet for long. The men were about to receive a baptism of fire. It was first light when the artillery barrage began. All hell broke loose around them at a time when they were supposed to be at stand-to- alert and ready for any eventuality.

'Fucking hell here comes the iron rations!' shouted David.

'We're in it deep now!' Archie shouted back.

All three men crouched at the bottom of the crumbling, muddy trench, with their heads between their legs. An engineer sergeant looked down at the three crouched figures and laughed.

'Come on you three, move out of the way, we've got work to do. Bloody hell, I can tell you lot are green. You needn't worry lads, those Whizz-Bangs aren't landing anywhere near here but you'll know about it alright when they do' the Engineer Sergeant said, lifting a sandbag from one side of the trench to the other.

In the trenches the soldiers identified shells by their size, effects or sound. Whizz-Bangs were fired from high-velocity guns and gave no one time to even duck. It soon became evident to the men that the Royal Engineers were by far the hardest working men in the army. Regardless of whether bombs were falling or not, they were always busy repairing, constructing and consolidating the trenches somewhere along the line. When they weren't fixing the trenches the Royal Engineers worked hard at reversing the captured trenches, even with enemy shells dropping all around them. These men carried out exceptional and perilous work throughout the war.

After stand-to, the men had breakfast and then carried out their daily chores, including cleaning latrines, repairing duck boards and filling sandbags, making sure they kept their heads down, out of sight from enemy snipers. Their first day on the front line was a very quiet one, which allowed the men time to get used to the routine.

The following day was Sunday and was also relatively quiet, apart from sporadic fire from the Hun guns and the odd sniper fire if someone was stupid enough to put their head above the parapet.

'It's Sunday today, the day of rest, so surely they won't be sending their little packages of joy over today,' said Bertram, making small talk as usual. 'And another thing I've noticed, the ladders, what are they for?'

'Bertie, stop being silly, you know full well what they're for. They are for when we venture over the top,' David replied.

'What, surely not... have you seen those rickety things, a man could have a serious accident climbing up one of those and get killed I'm telling you!'

'Oh shut up Bertram, sometimes I wonder about you.' David shook his head in exasperation.

'What do you think the folks are up to at home?' Archie asked.

David reflected for a moment before speaking.

'They'll be on their way back from church by now, then father will have his afternoon nap while mother makes the Sunday dinner.'

'Mmm Sunday roast, I could just eat that now, roast beef, roast potatoes and Yorkshire pudding,' said Archie, licking his lips at the thought.

Bertram started to whistle the hymn 'Onward Christian Soldiers.' Archie joined in and then so did half a dozen men along the front.

'Quiet down there!' shouted the section commander, Corporal Robinson.

Bertram's whistling continued for a short time until a huge explosion put paid to it. The earth heaved, shattered boulders and roots were flung into space, leaving a mass of smoking debris. A yawning crater appeared about twenty yards in front of them.

'Fucking hell, that was a big one!' Archie said.

'One hell of a Whizz-Bang,' Bertram replied.

Dear Diary,

This is our seventh day in the trenches. Every morning at first light, we come under heavy bombardment. The other morning, I was having such a lovely dream. I dreamt I was sitting in my Granddad's garden eating cakes and bread and butter when they started again. How inconsiderate of the Hun. I need to write a letter of complaint to the Kaiser.

Other than that, it's been a rather quiet affair. After our daily morning shelling, we spend most of the day repairing the damaged parapets and picking up empty cartridges left behind by the previous occupants, which litter the bottom of the trench, along with resting, writing letters home and cleaning our equipment.

The other day David thought it would be a good idea to boil water for tea, the smoke would show the Hun we were still there and not going anywhere.

They were relieved on the 27 August. On the whole it had been a quiet trip with very few casualties, but at least the men had been bloodied and knew what to expect the next time. After just two days of rest, the 10th Sherwood Foresters joined up with the 7th Border Regiment. Together they moved on to a place called Sanctuary Wood, relieving the troops of the 9th Brigade, from their occupation of trenches A4 to A1, on the 31st August.

Sanctuary Wood was very different to the trenches they had previously occupied. There was never a quiet spell here. There was always a constant flow of casualties, mainly caused by enemy sniper and shell fire. Before the war, the wood had been undoubtedly a beautiful place, but not now. The wood was littered with broken branches and bark, shell holes, wire coil and tree stumps. The smell of blood and decaying corpses permeated the air.

They weren't there long before it began raining bullets. Enemy bullets whistled over their heads or skimmed the ground in front of them. The men of the 7th Border Regiment and the Sherwood Foresters returned fire, but they didn't have any targets to fire at. If they didn't stick their heads above the parapet they'd be ok, it was the same for both sides.

'Damn snipers are everywhere, but you can't see them. I hope there isn't a bullet with my name on it out there,' said Archie, as he fired another shot.

'Yes, snipers abound, this place is a hell hole, I much prefer our last accommodation,' Bertram replied.

'I'm quite enjoying this scrap and it's not the bullet with my name on it that concerns me; it's all those other ones flying around marked 'To Whom It May Concern,' David quipped, ducking every time a bullet whistled through the air.

Positioned about three yards away from David, was their section commander, Corporal Robinson. David noticed he was showing a little too much skin to the Hun. David was about to warn him, when a bullet knocked the Corporal's helmet clean off, sending it flying towards the rear of the trench, about ten yards away.

'I can't lose my helmet,' said the Corporal, I've only had it a few days. Cover me while I fetch it, will you?'

David and the rest of the section looked on with horror as he climbed from behind cover and crawled to the rear of the trenches.

'Blimey, he must have a death wish!' cried Archie.

German soldiers turned their rifles on him and bullets whizzed around.

'Stop! You're showing off Robo, get yourself back in this trench!' David called out.

The Corporal calmly picked up his helmet and crawled back towards the safety of the trench, but just as he climbed in he took a bullet in his neck. They laid him in the bottom of the trench and did their best for him while they waited for a medic. His last words were, 'Damn the Hun… I got my hat back though didn't I eh?'

'You sure did,' replied David, as he tried to stem the bleeding. The Corporal lay in David's arms, his life blood pumping out of the wound. The Corporal gave a final sigh and was gone.

'Has he gone?' Archie asked.

'Yes, what a bloody waste,' David said as he laid the Corporal's body down on the ground and covered his face with an empty sandbag.

They all stood there, speechless. For most of them it was the first time they had witnessed death this close and personal. Every man present was affected by it.

'Time for a strong brew I think,' said David.

At any time, a soldier's life could be brought to an abrupt end by the enemy, even during quiet times snipers could pick off a Tommy before he knew what had hit him.

When the First World War broke out, the Germans trained thousands of riflemen to use telescopic-sighted rifles. The British nicknamed them 'snipers.' The word sniper came from the army in India in the late 18th century, when the officers would head for the hills for a spot of recreational bird hunting. One of the hardest of targets to hit was a bird called the Tiny Snipe.

Chapter 8

15th September 1915

The Battalion rested for five days at Reninghelst Camp, then they headed back to Sanctuary Wood for a second time on the 21st of September. Three new officers joined the Battalion to replace the officers killed the week before. This time a small scale operation was carried out on the 25th as part of a main attack on Loos. During the operation the wood was heavily shelled and the Regimental aid-post had a narrow escape.

They took over the trenches at first light and for most of that morning it was relatively quiet, allowing the men time to do some admin and write home to their loved ones. Later that evening, after being constantly badgered by his best friend Bertram, David finally wrote home to his mother and father.

My dear Mother and Father,

Just a short letter to tell you I'm fine. I'm having a great time here in Belgium. The weather is fine, although a little rainy at times, love the local wine, the neighbours could do with being a little friendlier. Archie and Bertram get on my nerves on a daily basis, but I wouldn't have it any other way. I hope Charlotte and Archie junior are fine. I can't wait to see the little chap and my little brother as well, hopefully this war will be over by the time he is old enough to join up. I would give a month's wage right now for a pint of beer in the Bridge Inn.

Well, I must close. Hoping to be with you all very soon,

Your loving son

David

PS. No rest for the wicked they say and if that's true, we must surely be a bad lot.

Later that night, after stand-to, the men stood around and talked amongst themselves.

'So, did you write that letter David?' Bertie asked.

'Yes, so you can stop going on about it now, it's done,' David replied, as he sealed the envelope.

'Isn't it strange Bertie, last summer I was all ready to start my new job until this all started, and now I'm here in this shit hole,' Archie said, sighing heavily.

'It's certainly a shit hole alright. More flooded trenches and shattered trees. At least there are no decaying corpses here,' answered Bertie.

'No, just well fed rats,' remarked David.

'Oh, we are a cheerful lot this morning. Cigarette anyone?' Archie began offering cigarettes to his companions.

They all took one, including the Platoon Sergeant. You could tell he was old school, he was always around when the cigarettes were being handed out.

'Never say no to a cigarette me,' Sergeant Johnson said, taking one from the box.

Archie lit up his cigarette and then lit David's with the same match. While the match was still burning Archie offered it to the Platoon Sergeant, who immediately blew it out.

The friends looked puzzled by their Sergeant's action.

'Never take the third light,' Sergeant Johnson informed them.

'Why?' Archie asked, chuckling to himself.

'Because young man, it is bad luck to light a third cigarette from the same match.' The Sergeant went on to explain why. 'It takes a German sniper about five seconds at night to see, aim and fire at a light source and a flaring match is clearly visible on a dark night like this from well over five hundred yards. Five seconds is about the time it takes for the third man to light up.'

'You know what, you're full of knowledge you are Sergeant. I bet you were a teacher before the war,' said Bertram.

'No, I was an undertaker,' the Sergeant replied as he walked away.

'Bloody hell, who'd have thought it, old Sergeant Johnson an undertaker.' Bertie was surprised by the Sergeant's answer.

'I bet it's frustrating for him, seeing all these corpses and he can't cash in on them,' said David, laughing.

'You're sick, you are David,' said Bertie, shaking his head in disgust at his friend's comment.

Archie stood listening to the conversation whilst smoking his cigarette. Glancing around the trench he became aware of a change in their surroundings.

'Have you noticed something Bertie?'

'What?'

'The rats… they've all buggered off,' Archie replied.

'They've probably taken cover mate,' said David.

'Do they know something we don't know?' Bertram sounded a little nervous.

After the war, many veteran soldiers swore that the rats could sense impending enemy shellfire and would disappear out of sight.

Dear Diary,

Today has been a quiet day in the trenches, the quietest so far, with very little shelling. I hope it carries on, but I very much doubt it. Now I am laying in my dug-out underneath my flea-infested blanket, writing my diary entry by candle light.

I've noticed there are two types of rat here, the brown and the black. I despise both, but the brown rat I despise most. It seems to be quite partial to human remains and it's always the eyes and liver they like most and some are as big as cats. I'm not afraid of these rats anymore; I've learnt to live with them. But what I do hate is when one scampers across my face in the dark. It's a waste of time trying to get rid of them. I've tried bayoneting them, clubbing them and even shooting the little blighters. It's futile. I've been told they can produce up to nine-hundred offspring in a year.

The following morning the Platoon were lectured by their Platoon Commander about an operation that was going to take place at quarter past seven that evening. The company had been tasked to clear a small wooded area to their front. It was a synchronised movement that formed part of the planned main attack at Loos. It had been reported by the previous night's listening patrol that the wood was only lightly defended.

The men spent all day in their trench preparing for the operation that evening, while the artillery carried out their usual preparations. This was going to be their first big test. Needless to say, there was a lot tension and fear amongst the men that day. At around six o'clock the artillery fire doubled its volume.

By seven o'clock darkness had fallen. The shells continued to scream over their heads and drop into the front of the wood, their objective was three-hundred yards ahead of them. Trees flew in all directions, ripped clean out of the ground, virtually destroying the enemy's line of defence.

Night-times in the trenches were busy, and more often than not, dangerous. During darkness, the men formed work parties, who carried out repairs to the barbed wire defences, dug new trenches and carried out strategic operations.

In the trench, the men of C Company were ready with their rifles, waiting apprehensively for the signal.

'There won't be much left of the Germans after that lot,' said Archie.

'It's not the big stuff that'll get them, that just serves to keep their heads down. It's the bullets, our bullets, that are more dangerous, so I hope you've all got your shooting eye in today,' the Platoon Sergeant replied.

Deep down, they all hoped not to meet resistance when they attacked the wood. Then the guns went quiet. The Platoon Commander looked down nervously at his wrist watch, like a coach at a football match, waiting for the moment, seven-fifteen exactly, when the platoon was to climb over the parapet and advance towards the wood, under darkness. The message came down the line to fix bayonets.

'Oh fuck, here we go, this is real isn't it, I'm not dreaming, am I?' Archie asked.

'Could you bayonet somebody Archie?' Bertram asked, shaking as he spoke.

'Well, we'll find out soon enough, won't we?' Archie replied.

'Oh, bloody hell, I'm shitting myself Archie.'

'I've actually shat myself, Bertie.'

'When we did the training all those months ago, I never in a month of Sundays thought we'd ever have to do it for real. To be honest, I don't think I could stomach sticking a bayonet into someone. I thought the bayonets were just for toasting bread, opening bully beef cans and killing rats,' said Bertie.

'Well Private Ward, you need to change your thinking pretty sharpish. Remember, right parry, left parry, forward lunge straight for the throat. That'll make their eyes bulge out of their heads. Left foot on the corpse and extract the bayonet, with a loud grunt! Remember that and you'll be just fine,' instructed the Platoon Sergeant.

'Indeed, but Sergeant that was when we were bayonet training against sacks filled with straw, this is for real. If it does come to it, I'm having a bullet in the breach. Kill him from two or three yards with a bullet, no personal contact is what I say,' Bertram replied.

'Remember what the training Sergeant said. EACH DUMMY MUST BE REGARDED AS AN ACTUAL ARMED OPPONENT' David added.

'Yes, he was referring to you Bertie,' Archie said, jokingly.

'Fuck you Archie Butler!' Bertram shifted from foot to foot nervously.

'Less of the swearing Ward, save it for the Hun,' reminded the Platoon Sergeant.

The bayonet drill was an important part of military training. Although only one percent of deaths in WWI were caused by bayonet attacks, they were an important psychological weapon.

Suddenly the guns fell completely silent.

'Why have the guns stopped Sergeant?' Archie asked.

'They are just adjusting their sights to increase their range, we don't want to be hit by our own shells, do we? Stand by everyone!' shouted the Platoon Sergeant.

The guns started again and this time the bombardment came from the heavy artillery. It was now seven-fifteen. After a blast from the Company Commander's whistle, they clambered over the parapets and advanced into the darkness. The barrage from their own artillery helped to keep enemy heads down. They moved forward, occasionally silhouetted by the flares and shell fire, some still smoking their pipes and cigarettes as a form of comfort. As they ran over the pock marked ground a few men staggered and fell.

One hundred yards from their objective the shelling stopped. C company quickly discovered that there was still plenty of Germans occupying the woods. The men took cover behind fallen trees and in craters. Then the fire fight began.

'Steady lads, get on a target before you pull the trigger, conserve your ammunition!' shouted the Platoon Sergeant.

Then the Germans fired a flare. Archie was in a vulnerable spot with hardly any cover at all. He was being targeted by a German sniper, five or six bullets chipped away at the tree in front of him. Archie prepared to move to better cover.

'Stay where you are Archie, I can see him,' David shouted, as he spotted Archie's persistent friend.

David waited for the German spiked helmet to pop up again. It was a clean shot to the face.

'Got the bastard, Archie, you won't be getting any more rounds from that quarter.'

The flare died away and they advanced further towards the wood, trying their best not to lose touch with each other. The men clambered over the rotten ground, under constant fire, taking cover again when yet another flare went up. This time most of the platoon took cover in a large crater that a howitzer had kindly left behind earlier.

The Germans were entrenched about fifty yards to their front. They tried to lob their bombs from their trenches, but they all fell short of their aim. It was now completely dark and the men of C Company waited for the signal to assault the enemy trenches.

The Germans sent up more star shells and flares, hoping to catch the British soldiers unawares, perfect targets for their machine guns but the British kept their heads well down. One brave German soldier crawled towards the temporary home of C Company to throw his bombs in, but he was spotted. He threw his grenade but it missed its target. He got up and ran back towards the wood. Unfortunately, he was illuminated by his own flares. He didn't make it back; a few dozen bullets made sure of that.

'Well, that was a wasted journey wasn't it? He won't be trying that again,' said David.

Everything went quiet. It became a deadly waiting game. There was no whistle this time. The plan was to wait for flanking machine guns to open up, to initiate the final assault. They advanced towards the wood lines under covering fire.

'Here we go again,' said David excitedly.

They fought like demons in the dark, watching for the flashes of the enemy rifles to indicate where they were. Bullets sprayed everywhere and men dropped all around as they rushed forward with their heads down and bayonets fixed. They fought their way through the deficient barbed wire to reach the German trenches and they were soon amongst the enemy.

'Come on lads, let's show the bastards!' shouted the Platoon Commander.

But no sooner had they set amongst them with their bayonets, most of the enemy gave up, some retaliated at first, but their stamina for a fight had gone. The German soldiers all surrendered, apart from a few who resisted, who they picked off one by one until there were none. The wood had been taken. The enemy came from the trenches, hands in the air, trembling, clearly showing the effects of the heavy shelling. Exhausted from the arduous fight, some men flung themselves down to rest while others kept guard over the prisoners. Their period of rest didn't last long. The shells started to rain down on what remained of the wood.

'Somebody must have been marking the fight,' exclaimed David.

'We need to get the hell out of here!' Archie sounded scared.

Just as Archie spoke, a huge explosion sent earth and trees flying. Detached limbs and body parts rained down around them, mainly from the German prisoners who had been blown sky high. The wood was their mark alright. The men were soon ordered to get out of that hell hole of a wood and move back to the safety of their own lines. The men frantically gathered the wounded and any remaining German prisoners and made their way back as fast as possible across No Man's Land. The bullets continued to teem down around them, but they made it back, although not without suffering further casualties.

Following their retreat from the woods, those who had made it safely back to the trench saw a figure emerging out of the darkness staggering towards them. It didn't take them long to realise it was a member of their own company, he hadn't been with them long and must have got cut off from the rest of the company in No Man's Land. He'd been badly hit by machine gun fire. His lower jaw was a shattered mess and he'd also been shot several times in his shoulders and legs, it was hard to believe he was still walking. He made it back to the trench and received immediate medical care. The soldier couldn't speak because of his injuries, but before he was sent to the field hospital, he wrote a note.

'I'm not sad, I made it back, some didn't. I'm happy we took the position and proud I was part of it.'

At daybreak the next morning there was a lull in the shelling that had been going on all night. Out across No Man's Land, the wood, which they had so bravely taken the night before, had been obliterated. All that remained now were isolated stumps to indicate where the trees had once stood. The ground itself was scarred and pitted, a cemetery for the unburied dead.

'Well, we made it Archie, we made it.' Bertram shook as he spoke.

'We sure did mate,' affirmed Archie.

'Would you just look at that.' Bertram indicated what remained of the wood.

'It's a bloody good job we got out of there when we did, or we'd have been mincemeat,' Archie replied.

'I've never claimed to be anything of a sprinter, but I bet I set a new record for three-hundred yards last night!' proclaimed Bertram.

'I wasn't far behind you. At least we all made it, us Derby fellas are a tough old bunch,' David added.

'David, you're bleeding,' Bertram said, sounding alarmed.

David's left arm had been cut open, down to the bone. Blood flowed down his arm and dripped off his fingertips.

'It's nothing, just a bit of shrapnel that's all.'

'All the same, you need to see the medic and get it cleaned,' Archie advised him.

'I wouldn't mind a few days billeted with those lovely nurses,' Bertram said.

'I'll not bother them yet. They'll be busy seeing to last night's injured.'

'Stop being a bloody hero, you daft sod. Go and get yourself treated,' Archie replied.

'How many did we lose?' David asked.

It was always a tense moment in the trenches when the roll call was made after such a charge. The number of missing men was revealed by the absence of their voices. C Company had lost fourteen men and a further thirty-two were injured. David left the platoon later that day to get treatment for his shrapnel wound.

A few days later, some of the men had to wear respirators because of the awful stench that came from the decaying bodies strewn across No Man's Land.

The following night it was their turn to be attacked. Sanctuary wood was heavily shelled again on the 29th September and a large mine was exploded by the enemy on their immediate left, followed by a small infantry attack, which was repelled. That same evening the battalion was relieved by troops of the 3rd Division and they withdrew to Reninghest camp. On their way back, they marched past the stretchered wounded and medics giving water to the wounded German soldiers. There was no malice. Amongst all this, sat the Chaplain, writing a postcard to the family of a badly injured lad.

The Bombers remained behind and were tasked to take part in a counter attack on the mine crater.

Dear Diary,

The place we have just vacated was beyond description. The dead lay in all directions, some from our regiment, some from the previous regiment who passed over this ground before us and the Germans. But the main thing is, all three of us are still here and safe. It has been a tough few days, the worst so far. David took shrapnel in his left arm and didn't tell a soul until I spotted it, he's either stupid or brave. I think it would be both in his case. I wish I was as brave as he though, he has no fear.

We are losing men at a rate of ten a week now. But that rate should slow down for now because today we are at Reninghest camp, for a well earned rest.

On our way back, we walked through a row of stretchers at the side of the road, on them lay their suffering burdens and it was the most moving experience for me. The enemy wounded lay alongside our boys. You would think after having passed through the ordeal of battle they would hate each other but neither bore any malice. I suppose both parties were only too happy to come out of it with their lives.

We've only been in the trenches a few months now, I haven't told anyone, but the strain is tremendous on one's nerves. When the shelling starts I shake just as much as the ground around me. At the moment I can hide it, I don't want to be seen as weak. Hopefully it will go away soon like the bloody Germans.

Chapter 9

Between the 2nd and 4th October, 'B' and 'C' Companies were used as reserve troops to the 51st Brigade in the vicinity of Verbrandenmolen. David returned from the field hospital and re-joined the Platoon after recovering from his injury.

'David, you're back,' Archie said, pleased to see his friend.

'Yes, they were going to soft billet me for a week until I told them I was fine. I looked for the medical officer and asked him if I could be transferred back to my battalion. He just stared at me for a minute, I couldn't understand why.'

'I can, I bet he thought you were mad! - Soft billet - you turned down a soft billet!' Archie couldn't believe what he was hearing.

'You know what they're going to put on your gravestone if you don't make it out of here. David Manning… he liked it here that much he never came home,' Bertram said, shaking his head.

David laughed out loud at his friend's comment.

Dearest Charlotte,

The parcel arrived safely, many thanks indeed for both letter and parcel. I've eaten the cakes already and the ham looks beautiful I shall have that for tea as there is enough to share with David and Bertie. I didn't tell them about the cakes.

Since I wrote my last letter, we have been busy. Do not worry, there hasn't been much fighting it's been fairly quiet. There is nothing very exciting to tell you apart from the fact we have all been working with the pick shovel day and night. I have blisters on top of blisters. We are only getting about four or five hours sleep a day. Last night we went out working with the engineers on work parties. My God those guys can work.

We have new lads turning up every day. When they first arrive, they don't have a clue how much danger they are in. One of them made a remark the other day that made us all laugh, he said 'Bloody hell it's boring here nothing happens, we just dig trenches all day. I've seen more action on a Saturday night.' He will soon change his mind. Now I must close, having no more to say at present, good night and God bless my dear.

Your loving husband

Archie xxx

In the trenches, waiting around for something to happen was probably the most fearful time. With not much to do other than guard and watch, the men had time to think about their loved ones back home and whether they would ever make it back there alive or even make it to their next leave date. Bertram was on guard while Archie and David were trying to sleep nearby.

'I'll tell you what, the architects of this dugout have got it spot on, apart from the fact that there's no door, but that can be overlooked. Just look at this roomy lounge area. No drawing room or parlour, but I'm sure the Germans can arrange the renovations during their next barrage. We haven't enough furniture to furnish it anyway. What really lets this property down though is the foot of sludge and the rats.'

'Will you be quiet Bertie, I'm trying to get forty winks here,' Archie pleaded.

'Yeah, give it a rest Bertie,' David added.

'No sense of humour you lot. I'm bored, bored, bored.' continued Bertie.

'Why don't you pop over to the German lines and ask them if they have any furniture they can spare,' David joked.

'I hate this place. I'm going to tell Sergeant Johnson that I've had enough and I want to go home,' Bertie carried on.

'Oh, I'm sure he'll be understanding and put in a good word for you with the firing squad,' Archie replied sarcastically.

'Why don't you do what that lad from B company did, he worked his ticket alright,' David suggested.

'Oh yes, I heard about that, but he had really lost his mind.' Archie said.

'Why, what did he do?' Bertram was intrigued.

'He was only caught by the Platoon Commander shaking hands with a dismembered arm embedded in the wall of the trench and talking to an imaginary German,' Archie informed him.

'Really?'

'Yes, what's the arm in that?' David and Archie started to laugh.

'Not funny David, you need to see someone,' said Bertram, who was not amused by his friend's sick joke.

Fear, boredom and the horror of the situation that the fighting men were in often bought out dark humour.

On 6th October, the whole Battalion moved into billets in Eecke and Caestre, having initially been told they would move down to Loos, but that move was cancelled. On October 21st, the Battalion was sent back to Sanctuary Wood for a third time, this time to occupy 'B' trenches. Apart from an annoying machine gunner, the main enemy was the infamous mud.

By now the men were familiar with the despicable Flanders mud. The trenches were full of sludge, sometimes as high as their gum boots. Some of them tried to scoop it over the parapets but it was no use, it was there to stay. The walls of the trenches fell in constantly and had to be repaired.

'How can they expect men to live in this, it's getting impossible to walk, let alone fight, in this mud bath,' Archie said, wading along carrying two mugs of tea.

'Let's all bugger off. The Hun can have this shit hole. Where's Bertram gone?' David asked.

'Sentry duty I believe,' Archie replied.

'What the fuck is this Archie?' David looked suspiciously at the mug of tea he held.

'Tea, Flanders special, drink up,' Archie said.

'It's got half of No Man's Land floating in it.'

They both looked out over No Man's Land, it was getting dark. There was only occasional shell fire and an annoying German machine gunner that let off a burst every now and again.

'Looks like there's a mist dropping, I wouldn't want to be going over the top tonight,' Archie said.

'Do you know something I don't? Nah, there won't be anything happening tonight, unless the Hun has other ideas of course,' David replied.

'No Man's Land is just a harvest for the grim reaper that's what that is. I wouldn't want to try my luck again. It's hard to understand what makes a man just leave the safety of the trenches and go forward into the sheer hell of gun fire,' said Archie, shaking his head as he spoke.

'Because we are fucking crazy, and the other reason we do it is because we'd be lined up in front of a firing squad if we refused.'

'Do you really believe that?'

'Yes, I do,' David said firmly.

'I think it's just scare mongering that's what it is.' Archie didn't believe the stories they had heard about men facing firing squads for refusing to fight.

Three-hundred and six soldiers from the Commonwealth were executed for cowardice or desertion during World War One, many of those were suffering from what is now called shell shock.

In another part of the trench, Bertram was lying down whilst on sentry duty. His job was to keep a look out for the Hun, in case they suddenly attacked. If he heard them or saw them coming he was supposed to fire a few quick shots to alert the men behind. However, instead of being wide awake, Bertram had fallen asleep. The big give away was when Bertram started to snore loudly, alerting the Platoon Sergeant who went rushing over to wake him up.

'Wake up Ward! And don't tell me you weren't asleep, I could hear your snoring over the bloody Hun shell fire!'

Bertram looked worried as the Platoon Sergeant moved closer to him.

'Do you know you could be shot for falling asleep at your post young Bertram? You were endangering the whole platoon.'

'Sorry Sergeant it won't happen again.'

Sergeant Johnson was a good chap and had no wish to put him on a charge. He also knew that the men had had very little sleep, food or drink. But he knew that he had to dish out some form of punishment to prevent a repeat performance.

'Go on, get off with you. Go and get some rest, but before you do, the latrines need cleaning.'

'But Sergeant,' groaned Bertram. Cleaning the latrines was one job all soldiers detested.

'On your way or I'll find something else for you to do.'

Later, after cleaning the latrines, Bertram rejoined his friends.

'Christ, what's that smell, is that you Bertie?' David asked.

'No, it bloody isn't. I'll tell you what though, the Hun must have blown up the local gas mains in the town, it stinks. I seriously need to bring it to Sergeant Johnson's attention.'

'What are you talking about Bertram?' asked David, looking confused.

'I've had to clean the latrines. Sergeant Johnson caught me sleeping. Well, I wasn't actually asleep, I merely had my eyes closed.'

'I can just see you now Bertie, with your Grandson on your knee,' Archie began. 'What did *you* do in the Great War, Granddad?' 'Well my lad, I dug latrines for other men,' Archie couldn't contain his laughter as he spoke.

'I hope you've left some of that tea for me,' Bertram said, noticing the mugs they both held.

David handed Bertram his mug of half drunk tea, as another burst from the machine gunner came whistling over the trench. The gunning went on for the next few hours.

As midnight approached, some of the men tried to snatch a brief rest, whilst others stood guard and fought to stay awake and vigilant as they observed to their front. David couldn't sleep, so he joined the men on guard just as the usual midnight barrage began.

'I hope they are our bombs dropping,' Bertram mumbled, still half asleep.

'Relax, they are ours alright,' Archie answered.

'That's ok then,' Bertram yawned and turned over.

Then came yet another burst from the German machine gunner.

'I wish somebody would shut that machine gunner up. I don't know what the bloody hell he's firing at, he can't see anything. There's no moon and it's foggy out there,' Archie said.

Bertram sat up, the constant sound of machine gun fire was getting on his nerves too. He glanced around at the men nearby and noticed that David was missing.

'Where's David? Has anyone seen David?'

'His weapon is still here so he can't be far away,' Archie replied.

Archie was right, David wasn't far away. Bertram, having given up any hope of sleep, looked out at No

Man's Land and could just make out a crouched figure receding into the mist.

'Is that David?' asked Bertram anxiously. 'He's just gone over the parapet and is on his way towards the enemy trenches. David come back you fool, what the hell are you doing!' Bertram called out.

David had grabbed his bayonet and begun his one man mission. There was no light, apart from the flashes of the German machine gun. David was now only a hundred yards away from the machine gunner's post. He moved from crater to crater, foot by foot until he was sidelong of the German machine gunner, who illuminated himself every time he pulled the trigger.

'I hope to God, he comes back alive,' Bertram said as he stared out across No Man's Land.

Archie stood beside Bertram, troubled by his brother-in-law's actions. Very soon they heard a noise, a squeal, a similar sound to the one they had heard from the wood back in England, when David had dispatched Shirley the pig. The machine gun firing stopped. Five minutes later, a figure emerged out of the darkness. Bertram and Archie both held their rifles tightly, just in case.

'Is that you David?' Bertram called out.

'Yes, it's me.'

Sergeant Johnson arrived to see what all the commotion was about and stood watching the approaching figure.

'What's that he's got? Bloody hell I don't believe it, he's only brought back the prize, he's brought back the bloody Hun's machine gun!' Archie exclaimed.

Archie, Bertram and the men were happy to see David back in the safety of the trench. Most men congratulated him for his successful attack against the machine gunner, apart from the Platoon Sergeant.

'I'll be having words with you tomorrow morning Private Manning,' the Sergeant advised him sharply.

'Come on Sergeant, men have done less and got a medal for it,' protested Archie.

'What for, stupidity? We'll see what the Platoon Commander has to say in the morning. Now get your heads down or get back to your posts.'

Later, after the Sergeant had left them alone, David told his story to his friends.

'I just wandered over, guided by the sound of the machine gun. Halfway across a flare lit everything up, so down I went and waited until it had fizzled out. I proceeded slowly, crawling with my head down, body and legs flat on the ground, like a snake. I crawled under their weak defenses. I could just make out a dark figure, I was inches away from him but he didn't see me. I just lay in the dark watching, waiting for the right moment. The gunner, a young chap, was busy firing his gun while his number two slept about three yards behind him. I crept closer to his number two, waited until there was a blast from the gun and then took my chance. He was easy, I sliced his neck wide open, he never made a sound. It was the gunner's turn next. He'd stopped firing. I just sat behind him, we both sat in silence, then he lit a cigarette. He called out to his number two, 'Mehr munition Carl' he called his name again 'Carl mehr munition' it was then when he realised something wasn't right and sensed someone was behind him. Just at that moment a vary flare went up. He turned and saw me. 'Gott in Himmel!' he shouted but it was too late, he squealed like a pig when I skewered him. I could see into his beautiful blue eyes. I watched the life drain away from him as I pushed my bayonet deeper. That last gunshot was his kiss good night. He was a goner and I was bloody glad of it.'

'Shit David, are you ok?' Archie asked.

'Of course I am. I'm fine. Is there a brew going?'

'David, will you promise me something, never do anything like that again. I'd hate to be the one to explain to your family what you did if anything ever happened to you,' said Archie hugely relieved that his brother-in- law had returned safely.

'I promise. The constant noise was getting on my nerves and I just wanted to meet the devil full on that's all... unless you lot had put something in my fucking tea? Must be the Flanders mud... it sends you mad.'

'Just remind me when this awful war is over never to live next door to you,' Bertram said.

It had been a great day, but they all knew there would be another machine gun to take the place of the one David had taken. Within hours there was, this time there were at least three more machine guns rattling away. It was as though the German's wanted to prove to the British that whatever they did they weren't going to win. That night they certainly let the British have it. The persistent cracking of bullets flying over the trenches was deafening, it even drowned out the noise of the artillery.

'You see what you've gone and done now David,' Archie said.

'Never share a trench with someone braver than yourself,' Bertram chipped in.

Most soldiers thought nothing bad would happen to them, it was always the bloke in the next trench who copped it. They hid their fear, only expressing it in diaries and letters home or sharing it with their closest friends.

The next day, David was called to report to the Company Commander. He expected to be punished for his previous night's solo excursion, but to his surprise, he was congratulated. Furthermore, he was promoted to the rank of Lance Corporal and acting section commander.

'We could do with more men like you Manning, that was an outstanding act of bravery,' acknowledged the Company Commander. 'But from now on no more of those shenanigans. You now have the responsibility of looking after the men under you, is that clear?'

Dear Diary,

We all thought we were safe today as we marched from the lines until a shell struck, killing two men instantly and injuring five others. Their injuries weren't serious though, but bad enough to earn them some time back in Blighty and temporary salvation from the threats of the front. The threat of wounding and death is ever present. Thinking about it, why worry about getting killed or injured when the reward is a ticket out of this hell hole.

Chapter 10

On the 30th October the Battalion was relieved from their post and for ten days they were housed in huts, close to Ouderdom, before being moved to Ypres ramparts to take up their posts as reserve Battalion to the 51st Brigade, who held part of the line until the 6th January. Between reliefs the Battalion got the chance to head back to the camp at Ouderdom, where they could have a badly needed wash and a change of clothes at the baths. On one occasion an eighteen inch shell dropped near the Cloth Hall and everyone scattered in all directions. It didn't matter where you were, you were always in the range of enemy artillery.

The next few weeks were relatively quiet on the front, with few casualties incurred. The only notable event was a gas attack on the Ypres ramparts on the 19th December. The men of the 10th Battalion, Sherwood Foresters, rested at Ouderdom Camp and moved back to the ramparts. Despite the gas which spread through the town and the constant enemy bombardment, the section occupied by the Sherwood Foresters was fairly quiet. That evening they were moved back to Ouderdom Camp.

Dear Diary,

Heavily shelled again today and more headaches. We were moving through town heading for the Ypres ramparts. The town was soon full of gas. Once we arrived at the front line, however, it was all quiet for a change.

The biggest enemy now is the mud. The mud in the trenches is getting deeper and deeper, we seem to be paddling everywhere in our gum boots and woolly jackets.

It's impossible to convey the mood of the troops at the moment while in these damn trenches, it is so depressing. The weather over the last few days has been atrocious, and I've never seen so many rats, millions of them. And the lice that torment us on a daily basis make our situation even more unbearable.

The fatigues for the Royal Engineers and tunnellers must be impossible and heartbreaking, morale has hit an all time low. But soon, we will be back in camp, it's amazing what a bottle of French wine, a letter from home and a good meal can do. We'll be ready to meet the devil himself.

As Christmas day approached, C Company drew the short straw and would be at the front for the Christmas period.

A and C Companies took up their front-line positions on the 22nd December and were to remain in their positions for a total of four days until they were relieved by B and D Companies. Over Christmas, the official word sent down the line was to refrain from firing unless attacked. Apart from a little sporadic fire on Christmas eve it was relatively calm. Christmas day was uncannily quiet, which gave the men a chance to receive their first present of the day, a foot inspection. Followed by a generous helping of medical supplies for the prevention of trench foot. There were some unpleasant smells around that day as most of the men hadn't had their boots off for days, sometimes weeks.

My Darling Charlotte,

I hope you had a good Christmas my dear, I would have loved to see little Archie opening his presents. I hope I don't miss any more Christmases, it's unbearable.

Today we are safely back in camp after spending Christmas on the front line. The weather is terrible, cold with high winds. No Christmas truce for us, the command promised hard punishment for any soldier caught fraternizing with the enemy. Where's their Christmas spirit? But we did get some fraternize because a singing competition broke out. At first light the Hun started to sing the German version of Silent Night, it wasn't long before we all joined in, it was I must say an emotional moment.

It was a quiet day and night patrols were cancelled, probably a good job as we all felt very merry. We had an excellent trench Christmas dinner, turkey, Christmas pudding, mince pies, fruit and lots of rum. But we were still kept on our toes. Bertie had prepared some special presents for the Germans if they did decide to pop over. He spent hours painting holly and Christmas trees and Santa Claus figures on our hand grenades. Well, it is Christmas.

So, no pretty lights, mistletoe, sharing food, party games or a visit from Santa Claus for us, but at least we stopped trying to kill each other long enough to enjoy our Christmas meal.

Great news, your brother David has been promoted to Lance Corporal. He had to report to the Company Commander expecting to be disciplined for something silly he did a few days earlier. And guess what? He came out of the Company Commander's office promoted, your father will be very pleased, but of course that does mean he can now order us about on a daily basis. What's new?

Still no news on leave. Everyone else is fine. David and Bertie send their love.

If only I could just put my arms around you, if only for a minute I should be happy, but as that cannot be dear, I must be content with the happy memories of days gone by. God bless you my dear.

Until I write again. Have a wonderful New Year and I hope to see you and Archie very soon.

Miss and love you dearly. God Bless.

Your loving husband

Archie xxx

All efforts were made to provide a suitable dinner for the men on Christmas Day. The loved ones waiting at home were encouraged to send Christmas gift boxes to the front, to ensure that the ones they loved knew they hadn't been forgotten by them, or their country. After an informal truce, stretcher bearers on both sides went out into No Man's Land to collect the dead. However, it didn't take long for things to get back to normal, it was business as usual the next day.

Dear Diary,

This damn German shelling, the noise is deafening and now I've started to have really bad headaches and spells of dizziness. I think I might have mild shell shock. It's a waste of time telling anyone. I'm definitely not going to report sick, all I need is a few day's rest. I think you just learn to live with it. I know I'm not the only one suffering, I only have to look around me to know that.

When we arrived here, our battalion was around eight-hundred strong, we seem to be losing around eighty men a month, either killed or injured. Replacements arrive every few days.

Trench life is just a steady trickle of death and maiming if you ask me. A poor chap next to me had part of his skull blown away, a sniper got him, we could do nothing for the poor chap. The horror of it, why did it take him an age to die? I've had a belly full of it.

After a few days of rest, C Company found themselves back on the front line again. David had been given a task by the Platoon Sergeant and so he went to look for his best friend, Bertie, to help him. He found Bertram sitting in his dugout.

'Come on Bertie, I need you to give me a hand, come on, out you get!'

'Go away David, I'm not on watch yet.'

'I seem to remember when we arrived here you said you would never crawl into one of those dugouts, you said it was like digging your own grave. Now look at you, we can never get you out of there, come on out.'

'Well, things change David, so clear off.'

'You can't spend the entire war in there Bertie,' David said as he pulled aside the sacking that covered the entrance of the dugout.

'Shut that blinking door! There's a hell of a draft in here! Give me one reason why I would want to get out my dugout. No, I'm quite comfortable in here with my friendly rat friends thank you.'

'Fresh rations?' proffered David.

Bertram was soon out of his dugout.

'Did someone say fresh rations?' Bertie asked.

'Grab your rifle Bertie, we've been sent to fetch the fresh rations by the Platoon Sergeant.'

'Yes, Lance Corporal Manning, three bags full Lance Corporal Manning.'

David just laughed.

Thousands of 'dugouts' were created in the trench walls, to protect the men from the shell fire and bad weather.

Getting decent hot food from the field kitchens to the front line trenches often proved impossible. Everyone in the trenches cooked for themselves most of the time, adding whatever they could buy or get from home, to the basic list. During rest or reserve the company cooks would do the cooking. Occasionally, meat, vegetables and bacon were cooked and sent up to the line by the 'steely eyed dealers of death' otherwise known as the ACC (Army Catering Corps)

On the 6th of January the 10th Sherwood Foresters were relieved and travelled by train to Houlle and Moulle, where they rested and trained till the 8th of February.

The men were ready for a period of rest, especially Bertram, who needed the time to get himself in better mental shape. Some of the men hadn't had a bath for weeks and it was profoundly evident. The air was fouled with the odour of dried sweat, smelly feet, creosol, chloride of lime, cordite, poison gases, rotting sandbags, stagnant mud and cigarette smoke. The putrid smell of rotting corpses in No Man's Land provided no relief. The stench of war was awful but the men became used to it after a while.

My Darling Charlotte,

The other day we got relieved by another division and we've been sent a few miles back from the front to a quieter place for a well-earned rest, or so we thought. On arrival we had the rest of the day off. Most of it was spent sleeping, then the next morning we were woken up early for a spot of physical drill and a run before breakfast.

The rest of the morning was spent doing platoon drill, musketry drills and can you believe it, after dinner we spent the afternoon on a route march. Don't they know there's a war on?

Thanks for the cigarettes and chocolate and yes, they are feeding us well. As well as can be anyway. On a usual day we get half a loaf of bread, bacon and tea for breakfast, Bully beef and biscuits for dinner, bread and jam for tea and bread and cheese for supper. Lime juice is served four times per week, and we get a rum ration twice a week. It could be better, but it will do for me. I should think it's more than the Hun get. In a few days after resting and training we're heading back to the front.

I've noticed Bertram is suffering with his nerves. Hopefully this break will help him recover. David and I have tried to talk to him about it, but he'll have none of it. He hasn't lost his sense of humour though! The other day he made a crude sign to stick in our parapet which read. 'OPEN ALL YEAR HUNTING SEASON, NO PERMIT REQUIRED.'

But don't you worry my love, the line is a bit quieter lately and only now and again do we get a shelling, I'm getting used to it now anyway. And as long as we all keep our heads down, we are comparatively safe.

I'm hoping soon we'll be told our leave dates, we've been here nearly five months now, so we stand a good chance. I am so looking forward to seeing our son Archie junior again. I bet he takes up all your time, give him a big kiss from Daddy. By the way your brother David and Bertram send their love. Well, I must now conclude…

Love and miss you both with all my heart.
Your loving husband

Archie xxx

During bouts of inactivity it seemed to the men that life in the trenches wasn't all bad, but the constant thunder of artillery in the background was a reminder that things could change in an instant.

Archie was on watch while David and Bertram spent some time sitting on their makeshift chairs, (ammunition boxes) cleaning their weapons.

'Have you noticed something David, the mud has gone, it's all dried up, maybe it's a good omen. No more swimming from trench to trench.'

'For now at least but it'll be back, you can count on that,' David replied.

'That's a shame, I was considering starting my own ferry service,' Bertram joked.

'I see Collins and Green drew the lots for leave, the lucky blighters.'

'Really, Archie won't be pleased, he was hoping to be one of the lucky ones,' Bertram said.

'I'm not bothered one bit about leave. I just want to get this war out the way, so I can get on with my life. If I'd been one of the lucky ones I'd have given it up to one of you two anyway', David replied.

'Come on David, you must miss your mother and father.'

'Of course I do, especially my mother's cooking, but what's the point eh, I'd just have to say goodbye all over again. It almost killed my mother last time. No, they can keep their leave.'

'If I got it, I probably wouldn't come back,' Bertram said.

'That's just stupid Bertie, you would be shot for cowardice.'

'No, stupid would be if I came back here. It would be like jumping off a sinking ship and heading for the lifeboats, only to turn around and get back on the ship, and anyway, they'd have to catch me first.'

'Where would you go, what would you do? You're no coward Bertie.'

'No, not a coward, just sensible. I'd probably go to Africa, no one would find me there. I'd live in the jungle with the natives, I'm sure we'd get on just fine.'

'What about all the wild beasts, such as the lions?' David asked.

'Oh, I'm not worried about lions. As long as I have a chair with me I'll be safe, just like at the circus. Lions are scared of chairs.'

'Bertie you don't half talk shit sometimes.'

'Bugger!' said Bertram jumping up from his seat. 'I was supposed to report to Sergeant Johnson. I'm on latrine duty again.'

Then Archie returned and sat on Bertram's vacant ammo box.

'Where's he off to in a hurry?' he asked.

'Who Tarzan? He's off to Africa to find his Jane,' replied David. 'Hold up Bertie, you forgot your chair - the lions will get you!' David called out laughing.

Archie was clearly baffled.

'It's a long story,' David said, still laughing.

'By the way, who won the draw for leave?' Archie asked.

'Have you noticed the mud's gone, Archie,' David replied, trying to change the subject.

Those days of rest went by quickly and the revitalised men were soon on the move again. On the morning of the 8th February, the 17th Division relieved the 3rd division in the Bluff and Hill 60 sectors on the front line. The Battalion took up the position of reserve at a camp called La Clytte.

Chapter 11

In early 1916, the Germans had the advantage over the opposition regarding trench warfare equipment. It was being supplied to them in larger quantities and their hand grenades, rifle grenades and trench mortars were more superior.

On the night of 13th February, the 10th Battalion, Sherwood Foresters relieved the 7th Lincolnshire Regiment who were holding the Bluff, south east of the Ypres Comines canal.

When the canal was first dug, the spoil was heaped on each side of the excavation and over the years a thin wooded area had grown on the mounds. There was also a large accumulation of spoil which rose up high above the level of the rest, forming a ridge. This ridge was known as the Bluff. The ridge to the south east presented a sheer face to the enemy. On the other side of the Bluff, the spoil bank sloped gradually, towards the north west. The high ridge, that faced the enemy, was peppered with sniper's posts. North of the Bluff, the 10th Battalion and the men of C Company occupied a row of trenches called Trench 31.

From their position, the men of C Company were able to completely overlook the German front trenches that ran almost at the foot of the Bluff. The company knew the next few days were going to be tough when the order went around that all ranks were to wear their tin helmets at all times. The trenches here were as inadequate as ever because of the high water levels and the interminable mud. The relief operation was a strangely quiet one, but the next twenty-four hours on the front line tested the fighting skills of the men of the 10th Battalion severely.

'Wow, what a view from here!' David exclaimed.

'Do you think that we stick out like a sore thumb?' Bertram asked.

'Yes, but we do have the higher ground and if we look to our rear we can see for at least ten miles. A great spot for tonight's illuminations eh Bertie,' David answered.

'No, the best spot will be at the bottom of this stinking, muddy trench,' Bertram replied.

The support lines were situated to the west, along with what was once a wood, now just a mass of tangled undergrowth and broken trees.

'I can see why this position is so important, better not let the Hun get their hands on it. That won't happen while we're here, will it Bertie,' Archie said.

'Definitely not,' Bertram answered, whilst tucking into a can of bully beef.

'Good God, what's that smell, we're not being gassed, again are we?' Archie pinched his nose as he spoke.

'That's the smell of rotting corpses, surely you're used to it by now,' said David.

'Thanks a lot David, I'm trying to eat here.' Bertram threw his can of bully beef aside in disgust.

'If you think it smells bad now, wait until the summer,' continued David.

'I really hope we are not here then,' said Bertram.

Later that day the shelling was renewed by both sides. The crash and thunder of the guns shook the earth beneath them. Trench 31 took some large hits, resulting in many casualties.

'I wish Fritz wasn't so bloody reckless about where he tosses his shells,' Bertie remarked.

David tried to make light of the situation. 'Cheer up Bertie, it will soon be Valentine's Day so just pretend those falling shells are Valentines cards or flowers.'

But Bertram didn't respond, normally he'd find it funny, but he just stared blankly ahead. A deafening salvo of shells exploded nearby, causing Bertram to recoil in fear. He dropped his weapon and put his hands tightly over his ears. David bent down to pick up Bertram's discarded rifle and handed it back to him.

David pulled Bertram's hands down from his ears and said 'look after this Bertie, it may save your life.' before he strode off down the trench to check on the other men under his command.

The evening was quiet with just the odd burst of shell fire but Bertram had started to shake again, this time quite badly.

'Are you alright Bertie? You're shaking like a leaf in the breeze.'

'It's just the shelling that's making me shake. I'm not scared anymore, but my body is a wreck, I wish I could exchange it Archie.'

Archie and Bertie looked over at David, who was sitting with his head in his hands.

'What's up with David? Do you think he's crying?' asked Archie.

'Maybe he is human after all,' replied Bertie 'Do you think I should go over to him or let him have his moment? This damn war is certainly taking its toll.'

'Best if you go over to him Bertie, you are his best friend.'

Bertie wandered over to David. Archie saw the two men exchange a few words and then Bertie rejoined Archie.

'So, what is it, what's wrong with him?' Archie asked.

'Nothing you fool. He's upset because he's just dropped his weapon in the mud after spending the last hour cleaning it,' replied Bertie.

Dear Diary,

We moved back to the Bluff today. I wish my battle was only with the Hun and not my body as well, which has now reached a severe level which I can't hide anymore. If I don't improve soon I shall have to go sick.

There is the constant smell of death about and the feeling that we are going to get bombed again at any minute. The Hun has been very accurate with their shelling today. It is a really horrible sight, seeing so many men die in just a few seconds. They are sending these young men, some of them mere boys, 'over the top' to face near certain death. There will be a very unpleasant smell here in the summer. I only hope we are not here then.

The posters in the town at the outbreak of this war were nothing but lies, I wish we were all at home where we belong, with our families and not in this wretched place. I can feel it's about to get much worse. When my time comes to cop it, may it be quick and merciful. I could always refuse to go over the top and end up getting shot for insubordination or Cowardice. Surely that's an easier way to go. Perhaps the real cowards are the Generals who designed this war. I wish I had never joined the army, we are like lambs being led to slaughter.

In1917, 'shell-shock' was banned as a diagnosis in the British Army and any reference to it was censored in medical journals. There were so many men suffering from shell- shock that nineteen British Military hospitals were devoted to the treatment of the condition. Ten years after the First World War, sixty-five thousand veterans were still receiving treatment for it in Britain. The treatment of chronic shell-shock varied widely, depending on the symptoms, the views of the doctors involved, and sadly also the rank and class of the patient.

On the morning of the 14t[h] February the division was subjected to several heavy bombardments from German artillery and from mid afternoon the shelling increased. The Hun was really laying it on thick and everything was going off at once. The bombardment went on for another two hours, then all communications with the front lines were cut. Artillery retaliation was requested but proved to be inadequate.

'Are you alright Bertie?' Archie asked.

Bertram was crouched down, rocking backwards and forwards repeatedly.

'What the hell is happening? Surely this can't go on forever,' Bertram groaned. He was crouched down with his back to the trench as shrapnel hit the earth all around him. 'I wish our boys would get their act together and give it them back, it's all one way.'

'I reckon they are about to attack any minute so get yourself up here Bertie, we'll look after you,' David said.

Bertram joined his friends and adopted his firing position. He shivered in the cold air, as he leaned over the parapet and stared out at No Man's Land through his tired and bloodshot eyes.

'Prepare yourselves men!' the Platoon Sergeant called out. 'The Platoon Commander said he will give you a whole shilling for every dead German!'

From the other side of the divide, through the gun smoke, emerged a suicidal charge in mass formation, which astonished them all.

'Crikey!' shouted Bertram.

'Well, you can tell the Platoon Commander, there's a few hundred pounds worth coming at us' David shouted out to the Sergeant.

The German troops advanced closer, fully intact, until they came within range of the rifles and machine guns of C Company.

'Here they come boys, give them hell!' David shouted out to those around him.

That was as far as the Germans got, it was sheep to the slaughter, they were simply wiped out. The first wave of German soldiers didn't stand a chance and neither did the subsequent surge of sacrificial men who were massacred by the overwhelming firepower that met them. The men of the Sherwood Foresters had delivered a knockout blow to the Germans.

The British Army was armed with Short Magazine Lee–Enfield Mk III (SMLE Mk III), which featured a bolt-action and large magazine capacity that enabled a trained rifleman to fire between twenty to thirty aimed rounds a minute. Eye witness accounts from World War I, tell of British troops repelling German attackers, who then reported that they had encountered machine guns, when in fact it was simply a group of trained riflemen armed with SMLEs.

The enemy infantry assaults had ceased but the bombardment continued. Any remaining soldiers from the attacking German troops took cover in No Man's Land or retreated back to their own lines, only to be picked off, one by one, by the British snipers and machine guns. The battle was short but it resulted in a scene of death and utter desolation.

'Well done men,' the Platoon Sergeant said. 'Stay alert, they'll be back, that's for sure.'

'They'll have to come with more than that to take this place,' Archie said.

'Did you see that? They were being killed by their own shells.' Bertram was shaking uncontrollably as he spoke.

'Yes, and shells that were probably made by their mothers and sisters back home,' Archie replied grimly.

The Platoon Sergeant was right, the gunning began again in earnest. What came next proved even more destructive. A continuous torrent of shells exploded and the men of C Company expected another attack any minute. Then it happened. At five-forty-five that afternoon, German tunnellers detonated three mines, one under the Bluff (which buried a platoon of the 10th Lancashire Fusiliers sheltering in an old tunnel) and two mines further north, under the 10th Sherwood Foresters positions in Trench 31. The result was utter carnage, the blasts had carved out a massive crater and destroyed most of the line in that area.

Archie lay in the open air, looking up at the cloudless blue sky. It was a hot August summer evening and he was back in the field at Parkers Piece. However, this time Charlotte wasn't there, no one was there. Am I dead, he thought, then something obscured his vision. With the sun in his eyes, he couldn't make out what it was. Then he saw a locket and chain swinging above his head... his precious locket and chain. Archie tried to sit up and take the locket in his hands. Then he realised where he was. He was lying on the rotten, swampy ground, badly injured but alive. He could hear a familiar, reassuring voice.

'It's me, David, lay down Archie, you're in a bad way but I'm here now and I'll look after you, you're going to be fine.'

'Am I dead David, are we in heaven?'

'No Archie, you're very much alive. Look, I found your locket it must have come off in the blast.'

'Blast, what blast?'

Archie's body was broken, he was out of the fight. He'd been blown sky high, as had his comrades, and landed on open ground. Archie was concussed, he had broken bones and a deep gash on his right thigh. Blood ran from both his ears. He'd also lost his tin helmet and most of his uniform had been blown off in the explosion, he was in a bad way. David was one of the luckier ones, he had only minor injuries, a cut to his right eye and a broken nose.

'Come on Archie I need to get you away from here.'

Crouching down, David reached out and grabbed Archie by the shoulders and dragged him for fifty yards away from what was left of Trench 31, then he set about patching Archie up with field dressings, that was all he could do.

'Archie stay here, I'm off to find Bertie.'

David had an impossible task because most of the company had perished. It was a horrific scene, body parts lay everywhere, but most of the men had been buried when the mine exploded. David needed to find his best friend. He began calling out.

'Bertie! Bertie!' There was no reply.

Chapter 12

A few weeks later, Charlotte stood on her doorstep looking both fearful and hopeful in equal measure, her face was ghostly white. She had heard about the mine incident and had been told to expect bad news because so many of C Company had been killed or badly injured. She watched as the postman approached the house, praying and hoping he would walk on by, but this time he didn't. The postman handed the telegram to Charlotte, the same dreaded telegram that he'd delivered more than a hundred times over the last few days.

Charlotte's hands visibly trembled as she opened the telegram. She tried to read the words but the tears in her eyes blurred her vision. She rubbed furiously at her eyes and began to read the telegram. The telegram slipped through her fingers and fluttered to the ground as her hand covered her mouth. Charlotte dropped to her knees and sobbed uncontrollably. Her mother, who was standing behind her, next to her father in his wheelchair, both shed copious tears when Charlotte relayed the awful news.

*****

David continued to search for his best friend in the devastated Trench 31 but time wasn't on his side. He knew that there would be an enemy attack at any second, it was inevitable after the firing of a mine. The Germans wanted Trench 31 and the Bluff. David was about to give up his frantic search when he came across a partly buried body.

He knelt down beside the body and brushed the earth from the face. The face that stared back at him with wide open eyes was one he recognised well, but it wasn't Bertie.

'Fucking hell Johnno, not you too!' David cried out.

Sergeant Johnson, father of six children, lay dead. David closed the sergeant's eyes gently before continuing to search for his friend, but his search was hopeless.

'Flaming heck, come on Bertie, where are you? What a bloody waste.'

Over the sound of shell fire, David called out his friend's name one last time as tears streamed down his face, but it was futile. He hurried back to check on Archie.

'Are you still with us Archie Butler?' called out David.

'Yes, I think so. Unless you're an angel.'

The artillery barrage began to intensify.

'Did you find Bertie?' Archie asked, his voice a mere whisper.

David paused before he answered. He didn't want to distress his brother-in-law further with his concern about Bertram.

'Yes, he's alright Archie, the medics have taken him.'

'That's good then, I bet he's giving them hell, eh David.' Archie's voice was growing weaker.

David had a decision to make, should he stand and fight, or retreat? He got to his feet, grabbed both his and Archie's rifles and slung them over his shoulder. He then lifted Archie onto to his back and started to walk towards the support lines.

'What are you doing David?' croaked Archie.

David didn't answer him. He was heading for the support lines, or as near to them as he could. Getting Archie out of immediate danger was his priority. The support trenches for Trench 31 were about three-hundred yards behind the main trench, providing a valuable second line of defence.

Breathing heavily, it wasn't long before David was too exhausted to go any further and so he laid Archie down and dragged him into a small shell hole.

'There you go Archie, it's a bit quieter here.'

'Pass me my rifle David.'

'This is not your fight anymore Archie, you've done your brave bit and I respect you for it. I don't want my sister to be a widow and Archie junior to have no dad, so you're staying here Archie.'

'David pass me a rifle.'

'No Archie! And that's an order. I'm a Lance Corporal, remember?'

'If you won't give me my rifle David, please take this.'

Archie held up the broken locket and David took it from him.

'Your sister will keep you safe, she kept me safe. Charlotte was right, you are a good man David Manning. Give them hell brother.'

David smiled, then reached over and grabbed a large piece of corrugated tin that lay nearby. He kissed his brother-in-law on his forehead and said 'goodbye Archie, see you down the Bridge Inn when we're back in Blighty.' David then covered Archie with the corrugated tin to hide him from the Hun.

David turned back towards Trench 31 to join the few remaining men that were there. 'Come on you German bastards! What have you got!?' he shouted out loudly as he advanced.

Soon after the mine explosions, the German infantry attacked again. The British front line was captured by five past six that evening and by six-thirty-two all objectives had been taken. All attempts to counter attack over the next two days failed. The front line and Trench 31 had been lost.

From the 14th to the 17th of February, the 17th Division lost one thousand two hundred and ninety-four men, including three hundred and eleven who were listed as missing.

Two days later, two stretcher bearers headed back from No Man's Land in front of the support lines.

'Come on, let's head back. This is the last one for today, the rest will have to wait, this fog is starting to lift. We don't want to join them, do we?'

The two soldiers lifted David's dead body onto the stretcher and headed for the safety of their own lines, but something made them suddenly stop in their tracks.

'Did you see that? That piece of tin just moved.'

'Watch out, it might be a German.'

They approached the piece of corrugated tin cautiously and then lifted it slowly.

'Eh Fred, we've got a live one!' exclaimed one of the stretcher bearers. 'Are you alright pal? Just stay still and we'll get you out of this hell hole.'

Archie was barely alive but he had escaped death.

A note was found in David's breast pocket along with a picture of his mother and father.

My Dearest Mother,

If this message should ever reach you, you will know by now that I am gone. Look after father and tell my sister and little brother that I love them.

You have been the best mother and father a son could ask for. I love you deeply. Just how much, you will never know.

Your loving son

David

Archie's injuries were too serious for him to return to the front and he was de-mobbed. Later that year Archie and Charlotte were reunited and three years later Charlotte gave birth to another baby boy, who they named David Bertram Butler.

David's younger brother, Michael, joined the newly formed RAF Regiment, on the 10th of November 1918. The next day the war came to an end with the signing of the armistice.

Chapter 13

Ypres Cemetery, 14th February 1966

David Bertram Butler stepped away from his mother, so that his father, Archie, could be with his wife to pay their final respects at the graveside.

He was buried alongside his comrades, sixteen officers and three hundred and thirty-four men from other ranks, all of whom perished in Trench 31.

Charlotte and Archie held each other tightly, united in their grief. They both shed fresh tears when Charlotte opened the precious silver locket, which had, for the last fifty years, held a picture of a brave soldier, her brother, David Manning.

Epilogue

Bertram's body was never found but his personal documents were returned to his parents via a German soldier, who kindly handed them over to the British Military. Below is a transcript of the letter written by my Great Grandmother, thanking the officers who called on her at home to deliver them.

Hillside
Chaddesden Park Road
Derby

Dear Sir,

I wish to express my very best thanks to you and to your brother for calling on me Tuesday last with news of my son, who has been missing since 1916. The unexpected nature of your visit took me completely by surprise and I am afraid I did not thank you as much as I wish for the trouble you have taken. It is very good of you to do so much, and I wonder if it is possible to get into communication with the German to whom my son handed his papers, etc.

If so, can you give me the name and address of this man, as I should very much like to communicate with him and thank him for carrying my son out of the trench, and also to see if it is possible to obtain any further information regarding place of death and burial.

I am,

Yours very sincerely,

Susannah Frances Ward

My Great Grandmother never received a reply to her letter and she died not knowing where her son's final resting place was. Bertram's name, along with so many others is inscribed on the Menin Gate.

Additional Information

The plan to retake the Bluff and Trench 31 started on the 29th of February 1916. All troops were equipped with the new steel helmets but the severe bad weather forced a change of plan. The bombardment eventually began on the 1st of March. By ten past five that morning, the infantry had captured all objectives. Counter attacks were made by the enemy, but the attacks were beaten off by British bombs. British casualties incurred during the recapture of the position amounted to 1,622.

In 1917 the order was given for twenty mines to be placed under German front lines positioned in Messines. It took nearly six months to complete and more than eight thousand metres of tunnels were dug. Six hundred tons of explosives exploded simultaneously at ten past three on the morning of the 7th of June, killing around 10,000 soldiers. The blast was so powerful it could be heard as far away as London.

On the 4th of August 1914 Britain and much of Europe were pulled into a war which would last

1,566 days, cost 8,528,831 lives and 28,938,073 casualties or missing on both sides.

The Sherwood Foresters Regiment raised thirty-three Battalions and was awarded fifty-seven Battle honours and nine Victoria Crosses, losing 11,410 men during the course of the war.

Lest we forget.

Bertram Allen Ward

The Regimental badge

SHERWOOD FORESTERS

NOTTS & DERBY

THE MISHAP TO THE TENTH SHERWOODS.

ANOTHER DERBY MAN MISSING.

Mr. and Mrs. Ward, of 135, Mansfield-road, Derby, have received intimation from a lieutenant of the 10th Battalion Sherwood Foresters that their son, Private Bertram A. Ward, is missing, believed killed, since Feb. 14. He was in the front line of trenches when his platoon was buried by the explosion of a German mine. Of the company officers all but one were killed or wounded. In civil life Private Ward was employed by Messrs. Vaughan and Son, tailors, of Derby. He was an old scholar of St. Paul's Day School, and a Sunday school teacher...

Clipping from The Derby Telegraph

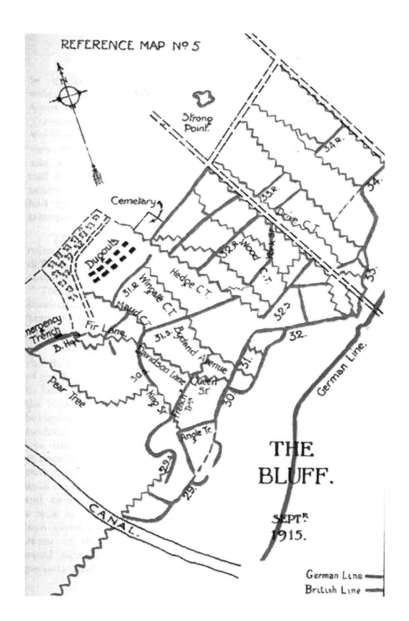

REFERENCE MAP Nº 5

Strong Point.

Cemetery

Dugouts

Emergency Trench

B. Hut.

Pear Tree

Fir Lane.

Naud C.T.

31.2 Winpole C.T.

31.3 Behind Avenue

Davidson Lane

Hedge C.T.

Queen St.

King St.

French Tr.

Angle Tr.

30.

31.

32.

32.2

32.3

32.R Wood C.T.

33.R

33.

34.R

34.

Dove C.T.

German Line.

29.A

29.

THE BLUFF.

SEPTR 1915.

CANAL.

German Line —
British Line —

A mine exploding on the Bluff, 14 Feb 1916
Picture taken by the Hun. Was this the mine
that killed Bertram?

Mineneinſchlag vor der „Baſtion"

Hillside
Chaddesden Park Rd
Derby

Dear Sir,

I wish to express my very best thanks to you and to
your brother for calling on me on Tuesday last with news of
my son, who has been missing since 1916.   The unexpected nature
of your visit took me completely by surprise and I am afraid I
did not thank you as much as I wish for the trouble you have
taken.   It is very good you to do so much, and I wonder if it
is possible to get into communication with the German to whom
my son handed his papers, etc.

If so, can you give me the name and address of this man,
as I should very much like to communicate with him and thank him
for carrying my son out of the trench, and also to see if it is
possible to obtain any further information regarding place of death
and burial.

I am,

Yours very sincerely,

Trench 31

.

Printed in Great Britain
by Amazon